OP: BELONGING

When Did Britain Stop Seeing Us as a Band of Brothers?

Samuel T. Reddy

Foreword by
Professor Martin Levermore MBE

COPYRIGHT

First published in Great Britain 2024
By TriAtis Publications (www.TriAtisPublications.com)

Copyright © 2024: Samuel T. Reddy

The moral rights of the author have been asserted.

All rights reserved. Apart from any fair dealing for the purposes of research or private study, or criticism or review, as permitted under the Copyright, Designs and Patents Act 1988, this publication may only be reproduced, stored or transmitted, in any form or by any means, with the prior permission in writing of the copyright owner, or in the case of the reprographic reproduction in accordance with the terms of licences issued by the Copyright Licensing Agency.

This book is sold subject to the condition that it shall not, by way of trade or otherwise, be lent, resold, hired out, or otherwise circulated without the publisher's prior consent in any form of binding or cover other than in which it is published and without a similar condition including this condition being imposed on the subsequent purchaser.

Enquiries concerning reproduction outside those terms should be sent to the publisher.

www.OpBelonging.com
Twitter:@opbelonging
Facebook:@opbelonging
Linkedin:@opbelonging

A catalogue record of this book is available from the British Library
Library of Congress Cataloguing-in-Publication data has been applied for

ISBN: 978-1-8382503-5-5

ENDORSEMENTS

"Op Belonging: When Did Britain Stop Seeing Us as a Band of Brothers?" by Samuel Reddy is a powerful exploration of the overlooked experiences of Commonwealth veterans who served in the UK Armed Forces. Highlighting the struggles of over 100,000 veterans from the Caribbean, Africa, South Asia and the South Pacific, Reddy captures their journeys from pride in service to disillusionment, facing financial, legal and social challenges in post-service life. Tracing a history that begins with the arrival of African, Indian, and Caribbean soldiers after WWI and continues to today's ongoing recruitment, this book is a call to action for Britain to recognise these veterans as true members of its society. Reddy's work not only brings attention to their sacrifices but also demands a "Reinvention of the Commonwealth Experience" so that their contributions are properly honoured and valued.

Professor Alaa Garad
Best-selling author of *'The Learning Driven Business'*
CEO of Dundee of Business Excellence
Founding Editor-in-Chief, <u>International Journal of Strategy and Organisational Learning (IJSOL)</u>

It is an honour to provide an endorsement for this empirical research which draws from past and present experiences and reflects on the future of Commonwealth veterans. This book uncovers the remarkable stories of individuals who, as heroes, sacrificed their lives to defend their nation, offering a profound insight into their journey. It also delves into reflections on resilience and bonds and offers a critical analysis of the complexities of military service and its impact on individuals. The book challenges leaders to reconsider the concepts of belonging and inclusivity in light of the honour and human cost associated with such service.

Dr Ana Paula Fonseca MBA FHE CSCMP PhD
Associate Professor in Sustainability
Programme Director MSc HRM
Deputy Director of Academic Quality, EBS Edinburgh Business School

"Op Belonging" embraces the legacy and the profound contributions of Commonwealth soldiers to the UK military which are brought to life with vivid detail and heartfelt respect. This book is a compelling reminder of the diverse cultural tapestry that has fortified the British Armed Forces throughout history. By embracing the rich heritage of Commonwealth soldiers, the UK not only honours their sacrifices but also strengthens the bonds of unity and mutual respect within its ranks. This work is an essential read for anyone who values the principles of diversity, inclusion and the shared history that continues to shape our modern military. A truly enlightening and inspiring tribute to the brave men and women who have served and continue to serve with distinction.

Lt Col (Retd) Michael Lawrence

This book will lift the veil on an issue that is under-discussed but has been pivotal in keeping Britain safe for decades. The contribution of Commonwealth soldiers in world wars and the continuing contribution of military personnel to the present day is only over-shadowed by lack of understanding of further contributions that these incredible men and women could have in our society. I look forward to understanding the history of Commonwealth soldiers in the UK military. I know that this book will expose many of the contributions and challenges faced by Commonwealth soldiers who are prepared to leave their countries to put their lives on the line in the defence of the UK.

Kul Mahay
Leadership and EQ Specialist: Public Speaking and Leadership Communications
Host of Human Centred Leadership Podcast
Director of Ignite Your Inner Potential

Your book's unforgettable stories deeply moved me, showcasing incredible pain and suffering. The individuals are true heroes in my eyes. This special narrative will linger in my memory. I highly recommend this book to everyone.

Dr. Abdoulie Sanneh
Director and Chair, The United Voice of African Associations (TUVAA)

As Samuel clearly explains, Britain has rightly faced criticism for its inadequate treatment of British veterans over the last century. Indeed, such organisations as the Royal Commonwealth Ex-Services League and the Royal British Legion were established to support individuals that served selflessly and loyally that were not initially British citizens.

Though these organisations (and many more) have worked tirelessly to close the gap between the needs of this large cohort and provision supplied, the reality is this gap is just as wide today. Even acknowledging the improvements in Government provision, many Commonwealth citizens who have served, protecting our collective freedom and security, still face multiple barriers when leaving the UK Armed Forces.

Harvey Tilley
Chief Operating Officer, Independent Living Fund Scotland
Co-Chair of Forces Children Scotland
Trustee of Community Veterans Support

I had the privilege of serving alongside foreign and Commonwealth veterans, and this book captures their remarkable journey with a raw, heart-wrenching authenticity. The author does an incredible job of portraying not only the struggles and trauma they endured but also their unwavering strength and determination. This is a piece of history that shouldn't be forgotten, especially as it echoes the lived experiences of many who served with honour. A must-read for anyone who wants a deeper understanding of the Commonwealth's contribution and the impact on their lives.

Neil Dean, CEO
British Forces Resettlement Services

I've had the pleasure of interviewing Samuel from day one when he started Op Belonging which seemed like yesterday. This book is very sad but shows how people can be strong even in very bad times. If you want to learn about history, read this book. It's very well written, but heart wrenching.

Richard Wyeth, Presenter
Producer, UK Bases, British Forces Broadcasting Services

DEDICATION

To my daughters, Alyssia, Alessandra, and Aurélia:
Your love lights my path.

To the Soldiers and families of the Commonwealth and beyond:
Your service to Britain through the ages has given me shoulders to stand on.

To my wife:
For supporting my crazy ideas and making this journey possible.

CONTENTS

Foreword 9

Note to the Reader 12

Introduction: Britain and the Commonwealth Veterans 14

PART ONE: A Cry for Belonging 23

Chapter One: The Forgotten Veterans 25

Chapter Two: The Forgotten Caribbean Veterans 38

Chapter Three: The Forgotten African Veterans 43

Chapter Four: The Forgotten South Asian Veterans 49

Chapter Five: The Forgotten South Pacific Veterans 58

PART TWO: The Hostile Environments in Britain 65

Chapter Six: The Right of Passage 67

Chapter Seven: Visa and Indefinite Leave to Remain 75

Chapter Eight: Getting British Naturalised as a Commonwealth Veteran Experience 79

Chapter Nine: Health and Wellbeing 86

Chapter Ten: Relocation 91

Chapter Eleven: Local Authorities and Armed Forces Covenant ... 97

Chapter Twelve: Britain and the National Health Service 101

Chapter Thirteen: Home from Home: Housing 105

Chapter Fourteen: Commonwealth in the Community 112

Chapter Fifteen: Education and Work Placement 117

Chapter Sixteen: Employment for Commonwealth 122

Chapter Seventeen: School and Childcare 129

Chapter Eighteen: Justice System 133

Chapter Nineteen: Non-UK Veteran and Non-UK Personnel 138

PART THREE: OP BELONGING 143

Chapter Twenty: Bula Festival 143

Chapter Twenty-One: Commonwealth Commemoration
Parade on Black History Month 149

Chapter Twenty-Two: Black History Month in the
British Military 159

Chapter Twenty-Three: Fiji Day 162

Chapter Twenty-Four: Africa Day 168

Epilogue: The Danger in the Movement of People 173

About the Authors 177

Foreword

This book is a journey of discovery, exploring the lives of those who have served in the military and their experiences after hanging up their uniforms. As Samuel and I delved deeper into this vast and captivating subject, I realised that to utterly understand it, I needed to look beyond the surface and into the heart of what was happening in towns and cities across the United Kingdom.

Over the past few years, I have had the privilege of working closely with several veteran groups and engaging in dialogue on subjects that deeply affected them, especially in matters surrounding preparedness for transitioning.

Is there a special case for us in the UK to identify Commonwealth veterans in the wake of the 'Windrush Scandal'? Whilst researching for this book, the overwhelming view from Commonwealth veterans was that the Windrush Scandal typifies a system that is deliberately stacked against them, structurally biased, and speaks more about the betrayal of a nation towards those who have given loyal service and personal sacrifice.

The Windrush Scandal has cast a long and dark shadow over many Commonwealth veterans, disrupting their lives and challenging their place in a society to which they have provided selfless sacrifice.

As Commonwealth veterans navigate labyrinthine bureaucracy to demonstrate their right to remain in the UK, they have been confronted with the stark reality of their vulnerability and marginalisation. The scar left goes beyond legal status: it cuts deep into their sense of identity, dignity and belonging within a country that they had once proudly served and defended.

Identifying Commonwealth veterans affected by the Windrush Scandal serves a vital public interest. The Windrush Scandal, which surfaced in 2018, exposed decades of mistreatment and oversight of individuals who had arrived in the UK from Commonwealth countries legally. Among those affected were Commonwealth veterans who had served in the British Armed Forces. Lest we forget, Commonwealth veterans have represented a group of individuals who have made significant contributions to the UK, often at great personal sacrifice. These veterans, who served in the Armed Forces, have fought bravely alongside their compatriots in many conflicts post-World War II to uphold the principles of freedom and democracy.

The Windrush Scandal uncovered cases where long-term residents, including those who arrived as children and served in the British Armed Forces, were wrongfully detained, denied legal rights, and even deported.

In the second part of this book, Samuel and I have tried to explain the emotional and sometimes traumatic subject of the 'Right of Passage'. It's a sobering reminder for me as a British-born person from West Indian parentage of the many privileges and opportunities that have been afforded to me. Like most British-born individuals, we so often take for granted the safety net and a common bond of 'place' to which we attribute our sense of 'belonging'. Likewise, we forget how hard those who have travelled to the UK have had to fight to call it their home and achieve the same sense of belonging.

Stories from past years include Billy Strachan who had to sell his prized bicycle and saxophone to afford the discounted £15 voyage to Britain during World War II. Such sacrifices continue today, largely unnoticed by many of us.

Billy's story: https://www.iwm.org.uk/history/war-to-windrush-and-beyond
https://www.iwm.org.uk/collections/item/object/80009824

Despite their service, many Commonwealth veterans have faced significant challenges in obtaining recognition, support and adequate respect. To identify and assist Commonwealth veterans cannot be merely an act of charity but more of a moral imperative rooted in the principles of equity, civility and gratitude.

The Windrush Scandal epitomizes systemic failure within UK society. This book seeks to remind our public agencies of their Duty of Due Regard when dealing with Commonwealth veterans.

Fair treatment of our Commonwealth veterans is crucial to rectify historical injustices. This book seeks to give voice to the contributions and sacrifices of these individuals, to acknowledge their legacy and to re-affirm our commitment towards building a more inclusive and compassionate society.

If we aspire as a nation to value all, we must not forget the bravery of those from whatever creed, race or colour. As such I hope this book contributes, even in a small way, to a more open discussion about the importance of structural and meaningful integration for those who have served us well.

Prof Martin Levermore MBE

Note to the Reader

This book brings to light the true stories of hundreds of veterans from Commonwealth and Gurkha backgrounds, with a focus on their lived experiences. As I lecture across the UK, engaging with other Commonwealth veterans, someone would invariably approach me after my talks to share their own experiences or those of a close friend. I understand that some events may be seen from different angles, with varying interpretations. As a military veteran with a Commonwealth background, I have witnessed and completely understood each of the experiences recounted in this book.

We have endeavoured to present those personal accounts in a fair and logical manner. Each of these little-known stories deserves a broader audience and comprises several interwoven tales. The first chapter delves into the lives of Caribbean, African, South Asian, and South Pacific Commonwealth individuals who travelled to the UK to serve in the military from 1944 to 2024 – identifying the shared experiences and enduring challenges faced by those who came to serve this nation. In another chapter, we explore their rights to remain after service, the struggles they encounter in integrating into British civilian society, and the consequences for those who fall through the cracks during their transition.

At the beating heart of this book is the cry for belonging. We unveil the mission of OPERATION BELONGING and how key organisations can play a critical role in the bigger picture. Together, we aspire to reinvent the Commonwealth experience in Britain and metamorphose these veterans into ambassadors, forging a golden thread between the UK and the Commonwealth of Nations. I have strived to encapsulate what each of them shared during our many hours of conversation. I trust that my recollection and writing effectively convey their feelings. While we may hail from diverse backgrounds, our 'Bond as Brothers' is perpetually intertwined through our lived experiences during and after our service, a testament to the purpose of 'OPERATION BELONGING'.

Introduction

Britain and the Commonwealth Veterans

On a summer morning in July 2023, the British weather once again decided to play its winter game, and the sky was not as blue and shiny but grey with a forecast of rain in the afternoon. Today felt different. In the last few days,] I have been talking to Mo, a military veteran of Fijian birth living in Scotland – and there I was driving to Bournemouth for the funeral of Livai Vota Boila, a man I had never met, never served with, and yet there was a profound connection between us. He was a British soldier born in the Commonwealth, who, like me, came to give his service to Queen and Crown.

You may ask: what was the link between Boila and I, and why was it important for me to attend this funeral? Little did I know that on this Friday morning after dropping my daughters off to school, that this funeral was about to impact so heavily on me that 'Op Belonging' was germinated.

My three daughters were all born at Princess Anne Hospital in Southampton, England, like most of their friends at school, but there is something about these three that set them apart. They are the children of a Commonwealth veteran who served in the British Army and, like them, there are over 100,000 children who have also inherited this legacy. Between all the Commonwealth soldiers that I had the honour to serve with, there exists a unique bond that makes them and their children special in my eyes.

So, what is the Commonwealth and why does it matter today?

What on earth is the Commonwealth all about anyway? This was the daring question posed by my 8-year-old daughter on our drive to school.

I was a bit shocked to be honest: she is my baby daughter and it seemed like in my excitement of raising her in England, I had forgotten to educate her about her roots. It turns out most children born from Commonwealth parents are pretty ignorant about this topic. Some children have no idea what their mum or dad did, or do, in the armed services. It seems like a taboo subject that they don't want their kids to be associated with – not in the playground nor in life.

It was in 1931 that the British Commonwealth of Nations emerged. The modern Commonwealth was later conceived as an organisation of 'free and equal members' that came into being in 1949 and was renamed the Commonwealth of Nations. It was built on the highest qualities of the spirit of man: friendship, loyalty, and the desire for freedom and peace; a family of nations. In short, the Commonwealth is essentially a voluntary association of 56 independent countries, home to 2.5 billion people and includes both advanced economies and developing countries. Before we discuss the Commonwealth veterans who served inside and not outside the British Armed forces, it is important to fully grasp the concept of the Commonwealth in the third decade of the 21st Century.

This concept of the Commonwealth has perhaps been the most difficult part of this book, because although the history of the Commonwealth is clearly written, its concepts are not very clear to many today. What makes it even more confusing, or even complicated, is the idea of the Commonwealth Games and the Commonwealth war graves.

Writing this book is my attempt, as a Mauritian–British man, to explain to my three daughters the reasons why they are here and, most importantly, the reason why I am here as a Commonwealth citizen who served in the British Armed Forces and the significance of this revelation to them as British citizens.

I am part of Generation X, born between 1965 and 1980, perhaps the last generation to fully understand the concept of the Commonwealth.

While this book focuses on the lived experience of Commonwealth veterans in Britain, it is essential to note the living knowledge of the British people about the Commonwealth today. To many of my British brothers and sisters in arms, it makes no difference – we trained, lived, laughed and some of us died in the most tragic ways. Make no mistake: most see us as one, and when you do meet them, they will automatically embrace you equally. Together, we are part of a family of over 2.5 million veterans living in the United Kingdom. Most children at school, friends at college or teachers at university have very little knowledge of us; in fact, most may not even know our stories. When they hear about the Commonwealth, some people think of the British Empire, while others see it as Britain's colonial legacy. Regardless of how they see it, this book is to enlighten them with a better vision of people who came and gave their service to the Crown.

In 1939, researchers from the Mass Observation project conducted an eye-opening survey about racial attitudes in Britain. What they found was troubling – most English people knew very little about West Indians and Caribbean people and, at best, felt indifferent towards them. During World War 2, the British Government promoted an idealistic image of a united Commonwealth family fighting together against Hitler. But for many West Indians who came to Britain to help the "Mother Country," the reality was far different from this rosy picture. When West Indian immigrants arrived in Britain, instead of finding a warm welcome, they often faced suspicion, discrimination, and even open hostility. The idea of a close-knit Commonwealth turned out to be more propaganda than truth. Sadly, the ignorance and prejudice uncovered in that 1939 survey have persisted in many ways, even 80 years later. Despite decades of immigration, cultural exchange, and efforts to increase diversity and understanding, many in British society still lack the knowledge about the connection to their Caribbean and West Indian neighbours and fellow citizens. The Mass Observation project held up a mirror to British society in 1939. Now, eight decades on, it's worth asking ourselves: how much progress have we really made in overcoming those deep-seated prejudices and bridging the divides between communities? Have we grown and changed as much as we should have by now? (https://www.sussex.ac.uk/library/special-collections/mass-obs-search/directives)

By 1950, the Central Office of Information in the UK produced a booklet titled "A West Indian in England," aimed at helping West Indian immigrants navigate their new lives in Britain. Written by H.D. Carberry and Dudley Thompson, the booklet provided practical advice and insights into what newcomers could expect upon arrival. The booklet addressed the issue of racial prejudice, noting that while there was no legal colour bar in England, social prejudices did exist. It reassured readers that they had the right to be served in public places, provided they were appropriately dressed and behaved properly. The booklet cited the case of famous cricketer Learie Constantine, who successfully sued a hotel for racial discrimination, as an example of the legal protections available. Despite the official stance against racial discrimination, the booklet acknowledged that prejudice was still a reality. It mentioned instances where private individuals or businesses might refuse service to West Indians, and highlighted the government's efforts to combat such discrimination where possible.
(https://www.nationalarchives.gov.uk/education/resources/fifties-britain/west-indian-england/)

While researching for this chapter, I rang my British-born friend David. He is married to Belinda who is Jamaican, and I have known them then since my eldest daughter was two years' old. David always wanted to be part of the RAF and the Cadet Force. I asked him about when he first learned about the Commonwealth at school as we are both same age, and if comparing his understanding with mine would it constitute good research. His answer was centred around his passion for stamp collecting and the *Encyclopaedia Britannica* that his dad bought him when he was about seven years' old. He honestly could not recall learning much about the Commonwealth at school; it was always associated with the Royal family and if you were into the Royals, then you would know more about the Commonwealth. This prompted me to realise that apart from Britain, I know nothing about the other Commonwealth countries either. This was confirmed when I asked the same question to Belinda – although she was from the Caribbean, and I was from Indian Ocean, we both had limited knowledge of the other Commonwealth Countries apart from Britain, our mother country.

I stumbled upon a pamphlet produced in 1961 by Her Majesty's Stationary Office, written by a group of H.M. Inspectors; this pamphlet made the case for more time for Commonwealth studies in the school curriculum. It was endorsed by Sir David Eccles, Minister of Education twice (1954–57 and 1959–62). Below is an extract from the introduction:

> *'Why,' said the Australian. 'do the British expect us to know so much about their history? None of them seems to know even where Canberra is or to have heard of Wilfred Lawson [*]. They don't know anything of the guts of the men – and women too – who cut their way through the bush and into the lonely sheep country out back.' And then, in changed mood, 'But I'm planning a trip to England next year. The kids are keen to see the Tower of London, and Buckingham Palace, and Westminster, and Stratford and, of course, the little place in Winchcombe where the old grandfather still lives.'*

The Australian expresses a mixture of affection and resentment. He feels that something is not quite right, yet his words imply a conviction that the bonds between Australia and Great Britain are strong and not lightly to be broken. At an informal gathering of Commonwealth visitors held towards the end of 1959 in the North of England, Africans, Indians and

West Indians spoke in the same vein. All of them had arrived knowing much of our history and familiar with the essentials of our geography, but all had found that we, in our turn, knew much less than they would have expected about their own countries. Some indeed had gathered the impression that our knowledge, such as it was, tended to be of the White peoples of the Commonwealth. Others maintained that what we learned of coloured races was heavily embroidered with descriptions of primitive conditions and tribal customs; that we were treated, like tourists, to picturesque details but were starved of basic facts about cultural growth and social development. Hence, they detected in our attitude a touch of patronage and not a little complacency. Nor did they consider that the literature, broadcasts and films available to those of us who sought to know more were likely to give us a true picture.

How do its people regard the Commonwealth? What is its significance for them? A Pakistani boy when asked this question talked gleefully of 'Big Ben, London and the Queen'. To him, these represented the heart of the matter. One of his more mature friends added, 'The Commonwealth, to me, is a kind of club, in which members of different colours, creeds and races may sit together in friendly and tolerant association.' But an Indian, writing from the centre of the Deccan, gave a very different answer:

'Frankly, our students here and elsewhere have no views on it because the Commonwealth idea has been driven out by other current ideas, viz. our relations with China and Pakistan ... The politicians think that, since Britain has ceased to be a first-rate world power, the Commonwealth idea is not as important as our relations with either the U.S.A. or Russia.' Meanwhile, from the other side of the world, a Barbadian adjusts the balance when he comments: 'Britain no longer matters, but the Commonwealth does.' And having said this, he pleads for a greater sense of responsibility for teaching about the Commonwealth in Britain.

The introduction goes on to say:

"Ignorance, complacency, lack of responsibility – these are harsh words. They suggest either that we take the Commonwealth for granted or that we do not really believe in it. We can deny both suggestions; we can as a nation refute the implication of such harsh words. But it is more difficult for us, as individuals, to maintain that the criticisms are invalid. We would do well to ask ourselves what we think of the Commonwealth and what we know of it, how much our children know and how real is their concern."

This pamphlet has been written in the belief that the Commonwealth, as a free association of sovereign, independent states, is a unique achievement in human history and that young people in our schools should have some knowledge of how it came into being and of its present significance. The pages that follow are an attempt to state, in more detail, the argument for teaching about the Commonwealth, to present a picture of the extent to which it is now being taught, and to suggest how this teaching may be developed further. Judged by any standards, the story of the Commonwealth is remarkable. It illustrates, on the one hand, pioneering adventures and achievements – whether in Canada or Australia, in Africa or India, in Malaya or the Caribbean. These adventures and achievements have been absorbed into the traditions of the countries in which they were enacted, while they remain an integral part of our own. On the other hand, it reveals complex traditions to which many peoples and many cultures have made significant contributions. These traditions will not survive unless all the peoples of the Commonwealth have some knowledge of each other and recognise the roots of their interdependence. You can read this whole 39-page booklet in the reference section. (Schools and the Commonwealth (1961). https://www.education-uk.org/documents/minofed/pamphlet-40.html)

As we fast-forward to 2024, it is clear that Britain is less significant as a nation today and as a single nation despite the wishful thinking of Brexiteers for a brighter future outside of Europe holding an ideological stance of its capability to extract better value and purpose within the Commonwealth family. As I write, The Commonwealth is a voluntary organisation of 56 member countries (Britain is one of them) with two newly added countries, Gabon and Togo, which were both former French colonies. The Commonwealth significance in the world for countries like Australia, Canada, India and, of course, America is much less than we could hope for. I have no doubt that the Great Britain we once knew is still trying to find its new position in the Commonwealth that is fast developing.

So, going back to my Introduction, what makes a Commonwealth citizen, and why is it that my daughters cannot be called Commonwealth citizens?

The modern Commonwealth was born out of its imperial predecessor, which, until the London Declaration of 1949, required all its members to retain the British monarch as head of state. Ireland left the Commonwealth that year to become a republic. India also ditched the monarchy followed by many countries, which in turn pushed Britain to agree to reform the Commonwealth we know today as a free association of independent nations. My own country, Mauritius, started the process of independence in 1965, but the island was finally ceded to its people in 1968 without the 58 islands and islets across the Chagos Archipelago.

Before 1949, Britain and its Commonwealth were a free movement of people until April 1949 when the new British Naturalisation Act 1948 came into place that would limit the entitlement to British citizenship. So, if you were born before 1949, you could be considered as a British and Commonwealth citizen. However, British Nationality Act of 1981 and the Nationality and Asylum Act (2002) separated the two with the statutory right of abode. The right of abode considers the country of birth and the nationality of the father and mother. This means that after this time a person born in Britain, or a British overseas territory, is no longer a Commonwealth citizen. Still, anyone born in a member country outside of Britain is called a Commonwealth citizen. In effect, anyone born outside the U.K. (except British overseas territory) is a Commonwealth citizen, but someone born in the UK is a British citizen. Is it that simple? I think not.

Today, as a single nation since Brexit, the greatest strength of the United Kingdom of Great Britain and Northern Ireland is perhaps the Commonwealth veterans who are the true ambassadors of Britain. As the next generation of Commonwealth children grow to become adults, they will be able to discover more if the Commonwealth member countries feel the same way towards Britain. In writing this book, I hope to remind everyone that Britain can develop its Commonwealth veterans and wake up to realise their association with the Commonwealth, or they are likely to become a small island in Europe like Mauritius is in the Indian Ocean. It was heart-warming to listen to His Majesty King Charles III's speech on the 70th anniversary of Commonwealth Day, where he described the Commonwealth as 'the wiring of a house and its people; our energy and our ideas are currents that run through those wires.' I cannot think of a more robust and appropriate way to describe my connection to the Commonwealth, and I hope it remains the most incredible reminder for all the third-culture kids with a Commonwealth heritage.

PART ONE
A Cry for Belonging

The Commonwealth as a Band of Brothers – when did it all start and end in Britain? Writing this chapter has been both inspirational and challenging – not because of the painful journey of Commonwealth history, but because of the rich tapestry of everyone who lives in the UK today, including those from the Commonwealth. One aspect I am tempted to talk about is the foods, culture and traditions that have been developed since 1944 from those who came from Caribbean, Africa, South Pacific and South Asia. Another aspect in my struggle to write this chapter comes from trying to establish what had happened. I needed to understand how it happened. Then, I needed to understand why. There is no limit to those answers – not when you have a history of 80 years to cover. Just weeks ago, I read that the Government has rejected crucial recommendations for guidance on the Windrush scheme. As I look at the Windrush Scandal, I can see an ongoing hostile environment towards my generation of Commonwealth veterans but surprisingly this system of treating people as second-class citizens goes way back to the 'Indentureship' system of 1833. What Britain needs is a root and branch rejection of the 'imperialist mentality' and a fundamental transformation of the system to make past and current Commonwealth veterans more welcome in a country they have fought for.

In this chapter we cover the three significant waves of Commonwealth generations in Britain. The first were the casualties of WW1 in 1919 who settled in UK, known as '*Dominions*' or '*non-Britons*'. The second wave took place post-War – also known as post-colonial immigration – from 1944 to 1967; they were known as '*Empire soldiers*'. Thirdly, the largest Commonwealth wave to give their service to Britain from 1998 to now, have been recently labelled as *'Non-UK'*. I will cover these in detail as per the immigration changes and subsequent Act that follows. Then, you will read about each of those who came to give their service to Britain: first the South Asians, followed by the Caribbeans, South Pacific, then Africans.

Each of these groups of people have their own unique set of values, culture, and identity. Belonging to a group is more than just following or leading – it's a deep, personal connection. It involves two key aspects:

1. The individual: the characteristics that make you uniquely you.
2. The social: the traits you share with others in your group, giving you a sense of belonging to a community, tribe, faith or nation.

Belonging is the bridge between these two aspects – it's how you as an individual connect with your group. In my first book, *'Leavers to Leaders'*, I focus on helping service personnel understand themselves better so they can reinvent themselves during their career transition. There's truth in the saying "you can't move forward until you know who you are", and a big part of that is understanding which groups you belong to. This sense of belonging is a fundamental human need. It's within this beautiful tapestry of different people and cultures that we find our *'band of brothers'* – the groups where we truly feel at home. Understanding your identity and where you belong can be especially challenging for those transitioning out of military service. But it's a crucial step in finding your place in the civilian world and moving forward with confidence and purpose. I realised that many people, especially those who came to serve this nation, perhaps do not realise the political minefield we all found ourselves in when it comes to giving our service to Britain. If you know the history then you may wish to skip to Part Two but if you gave your service and you have no idea what legacy you entered, then keep reading …

Chapter One

The Forgotten Veterans

So, when did it all start? To fully understand this, I am going to go back to 1944.

As I am writing this chapter, today is Africa Day around the world (25 May 2024), and I am about to head out to Farnborough Football Stadium to host an event. But also in a few days, we are all going to be celebrating the 80th anniversary of the D-Day landing in France, 5 June 1944. So, clearly 1944 is a significant time in the history of the movement of people to Europe to support Britain and the Allies. How was it possible for Commonwealth citizens (those who are born outside the UK) to join the British Armed Forces in those days? Well, the answer is clear: in those days, Britain governed a vast number of nations, as according to the "Declaration signed by the five Prime Ministers" in 1944, there were 5 members of the Commonwealth at that time: the United Kingdom, Canada, Australia, New Zealand, and South Africa. The declaration states: "We, The King's Prime Ministers of the United Kingdom, Canada, Australia, New Zealand and South Africa, have now, for the first time since the outbreak of the war, been able to meet together to discuss common problems and future plans." So, in 1944, the Commonwealth consisted of these 5 countries, which were all former territories of the British Empire and shared allegiance to the British monarch at the time. The modern Commonwealth of Nations as we know it today was not formally constituted until the London Declaration in 1949. But Britain also had a large amount of British Overseas Territories, for example:

In Africa: Basutoland, Bechuanaland, Gambia, Gold Coast, Kenya, Mauritius, Nigeria, Northern Rhodesia, Nyasaland, Sierra Leone, Somaliland, Southern Rhodesia, Tanganyika, Uganda and more.

In the Americas: Bahamas, Barbados, Bermuda, British Guiana, British Honduras, Jamaica, Leeward Islands, Trinidad and Tobago and more.

In Asia: Aden, Bahrain, British India, Kuwait, Mandatory Palestine, Transjordan and more.

In Oceania: Australia, Fiji, Gilbert and Ellice Islands, New Zealand, Solomon Islands and more.

So pre-1944, Britain did not directly call out for help from the Caribbean specifically for World War 2. However, according to a report in the Imperial War Museum, Britain did recruit personnel from its Caribbean colonies and territories to support the war effort, starting in 1941. (https://www.iwm.org.uk/history/war-to-windrush-and-beyond)

In this context, my focus is primarily the movement of people, and not the implication of the War itself. During that time over 10,000 men and women from the Caribbean saw the distress of Britain and took the long journey to the UK, serving in various roles such as the Royal Air Force (RAF), Army, Navy, Merchant Navy, as well as in industry, such as forestry and agriculture. This is the first time that non-British born people came to the UK and many settled here after the War. Was it an easy transition? Absolutely not. Did they integrate well and feel a sense of belonging to Britain? We know there are hundreds of thousands of stories, books and articles that covered these difficult times for those Commonwealth soldiers, sailors and aviators. In one book 'Small Island' the author described the life of a Caribbean wife living with her British landlord – quite a fascinating story of culture melting in 1948, which is eight years after the first wave of Caribbeans, and those who had a deeper connection with the West India regiments, came to support Britain in its darkest hour.

This is when the British Citizenship Act of 1948 came into existence. This put people born in the UK and the Colonies on an equal footing, consolidating British citizenship into a single status that included both Britons and colonial subjects. However, the Act was only marginally related to immigration itself and more about redefining British nationality in the post-War transition of the Empire to the Commonwealth.

So, in essence, the 1948 Act created a new statutory British citizenship that applied equally across the UK and Colonies, allowing free movement, in an effort to preserve Britain's relationship with the Commonwealth countries after they began adopting their own citizenships. This new Act gave access to thousands of Commonwealth people to come and serve the mother country. From my own birth island, search results show that from 1949 to 1968, Mauritius was a part of the 'UK and Colonies' Territory. Under Section 4, a person became a citizen of the UK and Colonies (CUKC) by birth if they were born within the UK and Colonies during that time (https://www.gov.uk/government/publications/historical-background-information-on-nationality/historical-background-information-on-nationality-accessible)

which would have facilitated migration of Mauritians to the UK during that period as British subjects. But I cannot see any evidence of this at the time of writing this book. I do however have a distant uncle who moved to Britain to join the British Army just before Mauritius took its independence in 1968. In fact, only five Commonwealth countries retained their independence until 1986, which gave their citizens a longer access to Britain. We have seen a longer movement of people from Belize, Brunei, Antigua and Barbuda, St Kitts and Nevis, and Zimbabwe. So, prior to those days, anyone was able to move and resettle in Britain – and then, in 1971 the Immigration Act came in.

Why was this 1971 Act introduced and was it needed?

As the world tried to rebuild after the devastation of World War 2, Britain saw a surge of new arrivals on its shores. The War had created a vast displacement of people and many found new homes in the United Kingdom, just as many British settled in Europe after the War, creating a huge gap across many industries. While Britain was expecting many Australians, Canadians and New Zealanders to come back, it was mostly other immigrants who came. One prominent group were the Poles. Thousands had bravely fought alongside the British during the conflict. In recognition of their valour, Britain opened its doors in 1947, offering them citizenship. By 1951, over 160,000 Poles had settled across the nation, starting new lives. But the Poles were not alone. To meet labour shortages; Britain implemented a guest worker programme that welcomed many others from Eastern Europe. This allowed sizable numbers to come and help rebuild the country's economy. The late 1940s marked the start of a new era of immigration for Britain. War-torn nations saw many of their citizens disperse around the globe in search of peace and opportunity. For those who made it to British soil, a chance at a fresh start awaited. (https://www.migrationwatchuk.org/key-topics/history-of-immigration)

In 1948, Britain passed the British Nationality Act, granting citizens of the British Empire the right to live and work in the UK. The Government's aim was to strengthen bonds with the Dominions – the semi-independent territories under the British Crown. Initially, the plan was to meet labour needs through workers from Ireland and "European Voluntary Workers" – the closest Britain ever had to an official guest worker programme. In fact, when the Empire Windrush ship arrived carrying immigrants from the Caribbean, the Attlee government had explored ways to turn it away or redirect it elsewhere. In his book, 'Citizenship and Immigration in Post-War Britain', author Randell Hensen talks about the Colonial Secretary, Arthur Creech Jones, who is said to have reassured his Cabinet colleagues that, although "these people have British passports and must be allowed to land, there's nothing to worry about because they won't last one winter in England."

(https://www.theguardian.com/commentisfree/2018/apr/22/windrush-story-not-a-rosy-one-even-before-ship-arrived)

Direct recruitment from the West Indies came a little later, driven by staffing needs in the National Health Service, London's transport system, and other sectors. Only about one in ten new Commonwealth migrants arrived with a specific job lined up. As the 1960s dawned, tighter restrictions were implemented on Commonwealth immigration. But this didn't stem the tide entirely. Despite the new rules, people continued flowing in from Britain's former territories, seeking new lives and opportunities. Britain was being reshaped by globalisation and its imperial legacy. What began as a trickle of newcomers became a current that would forever change the fabric of the nation. The 1950s and 60s rolled on: Britain witnessed a dramatic rise in immigration. With job vacancies aplenty and the promise of a better life, many made their way to the UK – particularly citizens from across the Commonwealth. Initially, these Commonwealth migrants were welcomed with open arms. But, as their numbers grew, so too did a sense of unease and resentment amongst certain segments of the British public. Fanning the flames of this negativity was Enoch Powell, a Conservative minister in the late 1960s.

The 1960s saw Britain grappling with the complex legacy of its Empire and the free movement of people it had allowed for decades. The Commonwealth Immigrants Act of 1962 had already started chipping away at those rights, stripping many Commonwealth citizens of their ability to freely enter, live, and work in the United Kingdom. But the 1968 Act went even further down that restrictive path. Its reach extended beyond just Commonwealth country nationals – it now applied the same harsh limitations to certain British citizens themselves. Those termed "Citizens of the United Kingdom and Colonies" who couldn't claim a parent or grandparent born on British soil suddenly found themselves shut out from their own homeland. No longer could they exercise that automatic right of entry to the United Kingdom that had been a core tenet of Britain's relationship with its former territories. Even long-term residents faced potential deportation if their family ties didn't meet the new criteria. The driving force? Fears that as many as 200,000 Kenyan Asians holding British passports might soon arrive on Britain's shores following their expulsion from Kenya. With bipartisan support, the Act was rushed through Parliament in just three days to close that perceived loophole. Declassified documents later confirmed what many had suspected: this Act was designed to restrict "coloured immigrants" despite advice it likely violated international law regarding citizens' rights. The 1968 legislation marked a pivotal moment when the "mother country" turned its back on the Commonwealth's people. It paved the way for the even harsher Immigration Act of 1971 that cemented Britain's new, insular approach to immigration from its former Empire.

Enoch Powell's infamous "Rivers of Blood" speech struck a nerve, voicing concerns that immigrants had no desire to integrate and that their presence would ultimately harm British society. While Powell was swiftly dismissed from the Cabinet, his words held sway. Anti-immigration and nationalist sentiments surged, becoming a central issue on the campaign trail as the 1970 General Election approached. With the public mood shifting, the newly elected Conservative Government under Edward Heath felt compelled to act. Their manifesto had pledged to tackle what was increasingly being viewed as an immigration "problem" – with a single system to control the influx from all countries, including a work permit scheme for Commonwealth citizens. The 1971 Immigration Act was their answer, following through on that electoral promise. It overhauled Britain's immigration laws, introducing tighter controls and restrictions that would reshape the nation's cultural fabric for decades to come.
(https://www.lawteacher.net/acts/immigration-act-1971.php)

As an immigrant from Mauritius who came to the UK as a student, Section 9 of the Immigration Act 1971 is what exempted me and thousands of Commonwealth soldiers and also Gurkhas who came to serve Britain. While most Commonwealth individuals will have this exemption stamp in their passport not many are actually aware of its origin. In fact, until I started my research for this book, I myself did not understand its full implications and consequences until now.

For the men and women serving in the Armed Forces, immigration rules often take a back seat when duty calls in the United Kingdom. Section 9 of the Immigration Act 1971 provides special exemptions that allow military personnel from certain countries to enter and remain in Britain without the usual restrictions. Take the British troops themselves – the sons and daughters serving in the Royal Navy, Army and Royal Air Force. Whether they hold British citizenship or residency rights, Section 9 ensures they can come and go as needed, regardless of their official immigration status. The same courtesy extends to foreign forces too. Soldiers from nations like the United States, that have visiting forces agreements with the UK, can bypass normal immigration control when stationed on British soil. Their counterparts in the NATO alliance also get a free pass under Section 9 for deployments and training rotations as we have seen with Ukrainians recently. And let's not forget the Commonwealth military ties that have been formed since 1919. The Act clears the way for service members from partner nations to undergo training alongside their British comrades-in-arms without facing immigration hurdles. In essence, Section 9 represents a gesture of military cooperation. By removing immigration barriers, it allows critical troop movements, joint exercises and knowledge-sharing to occur seamlessly between the UK and its closest allies. For these modern-day warriors, protecting national security takes precedence over immigration paperwork. When the call to service comes, Section 9 ensures they can answer it without bureaucratic delays. This is the reason why Section 9 is divided into 4 sub-sections:

Section 9(1) exempts members of the home forces (Royal Navy, Army, Royal Air Force) who are British citizens or have the right of abode in the UK. This exemption applies regardless of their immigration status, allowing them to enter and remain in the UK without restrictions.

Members of visiting forces: Section 9(2) exempts members of visiting forces who are in the UK by virtue of any designation under the Visiting Forces Act 1952. This covers military personnel from countries like the United States that have a visiting forces agreement with the UK.

Members of NATO forces: Section 9(3) exempts members of a NATO force who are in the UK by virtue of orders made under Section 8(4)(b) of the Act. This allows NATO military personnel to be exempt from immigration control when stationed in the UK.

Members of Commonwealth forces: Section 9(4) provides an exemption for members of Commonwealth forces who are undergoing or due to undergo training in the UK with British Armed Forces. (https://www.legislation.gov.uk/ukpga/1971/77/pdfs/ukpga_1971 00 77_en.pdf)

So, myself and the thousands of Commonwealth soldiers who have served and those still serving have all been exempted under Section 9(4) of this Act, and you will discover later in Chapter Two of this book how many people have been caught out when you are no longer in active service.

Then in 1981, the British Nationality Act came into force (also known as BNA).

In the aftermath of World War 2 and the winding down of the British Empire, the question of citizenship and belonging took on a new urgency. Just who could truly call themselves British in this new global era? The British Nationality Act of 1981 aimed to bring clarity to this complex issue. Its core mission? To reshape citizenship status in a way that accurately reflected each person's unique circumstances and ties to the United Kingdom itself. For decades, the vague label of "Citizen of the United Kingdom and Colonies" had applied to a broad swathe of people across the far-flung territories of the fading Empire. But as that colonial era drew to a close, a more nuanced approach was required. When the Act took effect on 1 January 1983, it amended the very definition of the "right of abode" at the heart of the 1971 Immigration Act.

In its place emerged a trio of new categories – British Citizen, British Overseas Citizen, and British National (Overseas) – each calibrated to better capture one's genuine connection to Britain. No longer would a singular, antiquated status attempt to unite those whose bonds to the UK varied so greatly. Instead, the 1981 Act ushered in a new era of citizenship stratified by circumstance and allegiance. For some, it granted the full rights and privileges of a British Citizen. For others, it acknowledged their historical ties while clarifying their status as non-Citizens. However imperfect, it was a monumental effort to reconcile Britain's complex heritage with its modern, post-imperial reality.

For generations, the term "British subject" carried profound meaning – a common thread woven through the vast tapestry of the Commonwealth. It was a label that united millions across continents and cultures under the British Crown's embrace. But as the sun began to set on the Empire, those ties that once bound so tightly were re-examined through a modern lens. The very concept of subjecthood seemed increasingly outdated in a world where former colonies had blossomed into fully sovereign nations. And so, a shift took place. The British Nationality Act of 1981 marked an acknowledgment that the old paradigms no longer fitted the new global realities. Out went the ubiquitous "British subject" descriptor that had applied to all Commonwealth citizens, regardless of their individual circumstances. In its place, a new term took root: "Commonwealth citizen." Two simple words that redefined the relationship. No longer a subject beholden to the Crown, but a citizen among equals. A part of the Commonwealth family to be sure, but with identities and allegiances distinctly their own. The paternalistic connotations of subjection gave way to the mutual respect of a shared history. With this linguistic evolution came the recognition that the United Kingdom's ties to its former territories could no longer be rooted in antiquated notions of the Empire. A new era had dawned – one that celebrated the Commonwealth's rich diversity while allowing each of its branches to flourish independently. As a testimony to this, one has to simply compare and contrast islands like Mauritius and Reunion (Sister Island) to fully understand the ruling and prosperity of these two islands. Reunion is still under the control of the French, while Mauritius gained its independence in 1968.

Since 1983, the UK has been using Section 9 (4) exemption like a tap to open and close recruitment levels from Commonwealth nations to serve in the Armed Forces, and imposes the liability to undertake Reserve Service if they don't complete a full service just like any UK-born citizen.

The 1980s ushered in a period of profound change for Britain's relationship with its far-flung territories. As the Empire's long shadow receded, redefining the bonds of citizenship became an urgent priority. Take the Falkland Islands, for instance. In the wake of Argentina's bitter invasion attempt in 1982, Britain moved swiftly to reward the Islanders' loyalty. The British Nationality Act of 1983 opened a pathway for Falklands' citizens to acquire full British nationality – a powerful gesture reinforcing the UK's commitment to this remote outpost. But even as one door opened, another seemed to close slightly. That very same year, the Act reclassified the status of Hong Kong's residents. No longer could they claim the antiquated title of "Citizens of the United Kingdom and Colonies." Instead, a new designation took its place: "British Dependent Territories Citizens." It was a semantic shift that hinted at larger realignments to come. While still retaining ties to the

British Crown, this reclassification represented a subtle downgrading of Hong Kong's status. An acknowledgment, perhaps, of the territory's unique circumstances and the delicate balancing act Britain would soon face. For while the Falklands crisis had reaffirmed the UK's resolve to defend its sovereign claims, the writing was on the wall regarding Hong Kong's future. The 1997 handover to China loomed on the horizon, a reality that British policymakers could no longer ignore. So, even as the Falklands Islanders basked in newfound privileges, Hong Kongers found themselves slotted into a citizenship category with fewer rights and protections than full British nationals. No longer citizens in the traditional sense, but not quite foreign either. It was a liminal space that captured the tension of that transitional era – Britain's struggle to reconcile its storied imperial past with an increasingly multipolar future. A future where the very notion of citizenship and belonging would take on new, more nuanced meanings. It was then in 1983 that everyone living in the UK had to register to become a British Citizen. Prior to 1983, anyone born in the United Kingdom was automatically granted British citizenship at birth. So why the change? Well, it was part of broader reforms to update and tighten the requirements for acquiring British nationality. The idea was to align the UK's citizenship laws with the principles recommended by the United Nations to prevent statelessness. It also brought Britain in line with many other European countries which had already moved away from an unconditional "birthright citizenship" model based solely on being born within their borders. In essence, the 1983 British Nationality Act took away the automatic right to citizenship through birth alone in the UK. From that point on, registration was required for babies born to non-British or non-settled parents, even if they took their first breaths on British soil.

So in 1988, for the first time, the five years residency restriction for the Commonwealth to travel and join the British Armed Forces was lifted, until in 2013 when the residency requirement was reintroduced.

However, between 1998 and 2013, Britain had to rely on the Commonwealth to boost overall Armed Forces recruitment, especially to demonstrate its commitment to diversity and inclusion from ethnic minority backgrounds, without them needing to have lived in the UK for 5 years prior. This was an intentional move by the British Government and Ministry of Defence. While no exact numbers can be obtained, it is suggested that in 2016 the Armed Forces had more than 7,500 Commonwealth citizens in its ranks from countries like Fiji, Ghana, South Africa, Jamaica, Australia and St Vincent. (https://www.gov.uk/government/news/armed-forces-to-step-up-commonwealth-recruitment)

When I joined the Armed Forces in the UK, I was already a student at the time, but I had absolutely no idea what was really going on in the bigger scale of things. Meanwhile, across the Commonwealth, a major military recruitment campaign was taking place in Fiji, Africa and the Caribbean for the British Army. We will hear more about the experience of those who joined with me as well as their experience after giving their service to the Crown in Part Two of this book. This residential requirement and non-residential requirement for many was seen as a strategic move by the British military, along with the limited options for Commonwealth recruits to access wider career prospects. As such, many who joined with me were not able to apply for key jobs across the British Army and the Royal Navy due to the residency requirement for security clearance. Historically, until recently, Commonwealth soldiers had limited access to apply for an officer's role – although some of us were better qualified than our officers, this was not an option on the table. I have met many Commonwealth soldiers with degrees and working life experience who were stuck in the Infantry role as non-commissioning officers; many are now veterans.

Although this chapter can be tedious at times to read, my hope is that it gives you a complete chronological time-stamp in the life of

Commonwealth soldiers who served before me and the complexity of immigration and naturalisation rules that have been wired around us – from free movement to the UK before 1971, to the rules around being a British citizen and Commonwealth citizen after 1983. I think these rules are fundamental for the future of our children who are British-born to understand their rights by our service to the Crown and to ensure they have a sense of belonging. For the rest of us, we are perhaps the only generation to be known as Commonwealth citizens: a term that is being replaced by Non-UK veterans and Non-UK personnel. More on this later.

Timeline of Immigration Rules for Commonwealth Citizens

1931 – British Commonwealth of Nations emerged
1948 – British Nationality Act
1949 – British Commonwealth of Nations renamed Commonwealth of Nations
1962 – Commonwealth Immigration Act
1971 – Immigration Act Section 9(1) – exempts members of the HM Forces
   Section 9(2) - exempts members of visiting forces
   Section (3) - exempts members of NATO forces
   Section (4) - exempts members of Commonwealth Forces
1981 – British Nationality Act – Amended the right of abode and separated British & Commonwealth
1988 – Five years' residency for Commonwealth lifted to join HM Forces
2002 – Asylum Act introduced
2013 – Five years residency requirement reintroduced
2018 – Five years residency lifted with yearly quota on recruitment
2024 – Major campaign to recruit Commonwealth citizens to fill quota of diversity

Chapter Two

The Forgotten Caribbean Veterans

"It is remarkable that events like this have not become a national outcry and exposition to what we have contributed. And to this end, I leave it to your good leaders to take this on board, so that our children, especially those who are born from Christian descent, should know that their forefathers made a contribution to the greater good of democracy and peace and tranquillity toward the world. I thank you." Neil Flannagan MBE (R.I.P. May 1924 – March 2024)

Who was the man – and how come this was the first time I had heard of him? His 20-second message was like a sniper shot that went out and quietly hit its target without much noise. I remember talking with one other person from the British Legion on that day when I spotted Neil walking in with the help of another gentleman, also from the Caribbean, who himself looked like a veteran with an injury. He and Neil had to make a massive effort to walk on the uneven grass of Southampton Hollybook Cemetery. I had no idea who he was. Then, another gentleman from a Caribbean background came in to support them and stood next to Neil; he was wearing a beret with a cap badge that I could not really understand. I was later introduced to this new gentleman by one of my Jamaican brothers, Ramon, who is still in service. Paul (the gentleman who stood next to Mr Flanagan) is the Chairman of the West India Regiment and runs The British West India Regiments Heritage Trust (BWIRHT), a charity founded by Neil Flanagan MBE after his service in the RAF during WW2. This small encounter prompted me to research the history of Neil Flanagan, who left us earlier this year at the age of 99. Neil Flanagan was a highly respected member of the West India Regiment, known for his dedication and service during World War 2.

His contributions to the regiment and his advocacy for Commonwealth personnel are significant and should not be forgotten.

The West India Regiment was an infantry unit of the British Army formed in 1795 to defend Britain's Caribbean colonies. Comprised mainly of soldiers of African and Afro-Caribbean descent, the regiment participated in various campaigns and conflicts until it was disbanded in 1927 due to economic reasons. In 1958, following the creation of the Federation of the West Indies, the West India Regiment was reinstated with three battalions. However, it was disbanded again in 1962 when the West Indies Federation dissolved.

Despite the disbandment of the West India Regiment, many Caribbean citizens continued to serve in the British Armed Forces, especially during times of war. Notably, Norman Manley, the former Prime Minister of Jamaica, served in the British military during World War 1. Norman Manley's experience in the Royal Field Artillery, alongside his younger brother who tragically lost his life during the War, showcased his courage and bravery. He was awarded the Military Medal for his acts of bravery in the face of the enemy.

It is likely that Manley's military service greatly influenced his leadership qualities and instilled a sense of discipline that served him well in his future political career. The experiences of war can shape leadership skills, such as the ability to make quick decisions under pressure and inspire others. Additionally, military service instils a strong sense of discipline, essential for navigating the complexities of politics and achieving national goals.

Manley's time in the trenches during World War 1 undoubtedly honed his leadership abilities and instilled in him a sense of discipline that proved crucial during his tenure as the Premier of Jamaica. His military experience played a significant role in shaping the leadership qualities that made him a respected and influential figure in Jamaica's journey towards independence.

On the afternoon of 8 May 2019, a member of the Scottish Parliament for Glasgow, made this poignant statement:

"We often speak in this place about the need to support veterans and their families after they have served our country. However, there is now clear evidence that the Commonwealth personnel serving in the Armed Forces are being left behind ... It is a duty of this and any Government to support all those who serve in the Armed Forces, including those from Commonwealth nations who serve with distinction alongside their comrades from the UK and Ireland. Commonwealth citizens have long made significant contributions to the defence of the United Kingdom, including during the First and Second World Wars. They continue to play an important role in the UK Armed Forces, serving in operations worldwide.
(https://hansard.parliament.uk/commons/2019-05-08/debates/3468AACC-1059-41E2-821F-EA20D21754FD/CommonwealthPersonnelInTheArmedForces)"

Although this was quite a powerful and compelling statement, in the next five years that followed we did not see much progress in this area. So, what prompted this statement? Was it the idea that crops up sometimes when I ask people: what do they understand by the Commonwealth; that it means those citizens have some kind of citizenship? If that is the case, then just take a look at what happened to thousands of Commonwealth citizens in the Windrush Scandal. Many of them served in the British Armed Forces and found themselves facing deportation to countries they barely knew due to immigration legislation.

In the next few chapters, I want to elaborate a bit more in the individuality of each of those personnel – we are, after all, from 54 countries and organisations do like to put us all in one basket. When I think of it, it is like saying that English and Scottish citizens are the same. Although I am a Commonwealth citizen of two countries, being

Mauritian and living an English way of life as a British citizen, gives me three distinct identities. I like to explain this by the way I feel when at airports: while I may behave in an English way leaving Edinburgh Airport for Mauritius, the minute I land at Sir Seewoosagur Ramgoolam Airport in Mauritius, I am in a completely different mindset. In the next few chapters, we will look at the history of key Commonwealth countries and their contribution to Britain.

Undoubtedly, the first cohort of Commonwealth veterans to settle in the UK are our forgotten comrades from the Caribbean. The Caribbean is made up of 28 sovereign states and dependent territories that are considered part of the Caribbean region. Jamaica is the largest island in the Caribbean that is part of the Commonwealth nations. My first encounter with a citizen from Jamaica was during my Phase One basic training in Litchfield. Ricky Morgan was my best buddy during training – until that time, I knew very little about Jamaica except for the famous reggae singer, Bob Marley, who rose to international fame and recognition in the early to mid-1970s with his band 'The Wailers' that propelled him to global recognition. This is also where the fusion of sega-reggae (a.k.a. seggae) started in Mauritius. The Caribbean has a similar colonial history to Mauritius, especially when it comes to slavery which was later replaced by indentured labourers. But here in the UK, most Jamaicans arrived by boats from Tilbury and Southampton ports and settled in London, Croydon and the Midlands. We need to remember that the first Commonwealth people to come and fight for Britain and live in the UK after 1944 were 6,000 Caribbeans and 3,500 of them were from Jamaica. This was after they heard the second call for help from Churchill during WW2 in 1944; the first call for help was from King George himself during WW1.

So, meeting my first Jamaican brother, with a very British name, was a pleasure: this felt very relatable to the same history that African Mauritians inherited from their French masters in the 1800s. Ricky

Morgan and I would often find ourselves reminiscing about life on our islands. It was so much fun and together we surmounted so many training difficulties in this new training place one hour away from Birmingham, the second largest city in the UK. It is sad that I lost touch with him. Ricky was a very friendly Jamaican, cheerful and always with a smile, and very popular when out and about, with similar height and build as me. We were both older than the average recruits: the British Army historically would recruit young Northerners at the time, who came from lower income backgrounds and council estates, and build them up not just as soldiers but as leaders who could lead during a difficult time. Ricky and I, being in our mid-twenties, had to make an effort to blend in as a team, get our mile-and-a-half under eight minutes, and keep our heads up, as we were trained by a platoon of Paras, elite soldiers. Any Commonwealth person who enlisted before me would agree that there is a lot to take in during basic training. I have no doubt however that people like Neil Flannagan and many others paved the way for us in Britain, not an easy time by any means and we will cover this later in this book. But his speech is one of the most eloquent in under 20 seconds that will stay with me forever.

You can watch his message on my YouTube channel in the show-notes at the back.

Chapter Three

The Forgotten African Veterans

When you grow up on a small island 30 x 60 km long in the middle of the Indian Ocean, life can be tedious. This was me at 18: I had always been looking for a way off the Island of Mauritius. So eventually, at 19, my best friend and I got off the island and headed to Africa and Asia. After all, when you look up in Mauritius, you don't see Europe but Africa. Eventually, when I joined the British Army, I met with my African brothers from East Africa, West Africa and South Africa; also remembering those inland like Zimbabwe and Malawi. My first contact with an African in the British Army was in 2001 during my Phase Two training: Afu was from Ghana. As well as growing up on an island on the east coast of Africa, I had diligently studied Ghanaian history and culture.

I remember us having a talk about a typical day in Ghana: When you come to my village on a Sunday, your nostrils are greeted by the medley smell of aromas wafting through the air. The pungent scent of fermented corn mingles with the savoury notes of fried onions, while the briny essence of dried shrimp and the rich, earthy smell of palm oil create an olfactory tapestry that can be detected from miles away. In the heart of a modest kitchen, you'll find my mother, a picture of traditional grace, perched on a low Ashanti stool. Like countless women before her, she's engaged in the time-honoured ritual of pounding fufu – a starchy, glutinous dumpling that forms the cornerstone of many Ghanaian meals. The rhythmic thud of the pestle against the mortar creates a soothing backdrop to the day's activities. This labour of love will soon yield a comforting meal, to be eaten by hand and used to scoop up generous portions of spicy, oily, and watery soup, a perfect complement to the dense fufu. Food, it seems, is the lifeblood of my village. It's not uncommon for relatives to materialise unannounced, drawn perhaps by the tantalising aromas or simply the promise of companionship. Some come to sit and talk, sharing news and gossip, while others might extend their stay, seamlessly integrating into the ebb and flow of village life. The weekends follow a predictable yet cherished pattern. Saturdays are a whirlwind of social engagements – joyous weddings, hopeful christenings, and solemn funerals – each marking significant milestones in the community's collective journey. Sundays, by contrast, are reserved for spiritual nourishment, with families donning their finest attire to attend church services.

This rich tapestry of village life stands in contrast to the experiences of many Ghanaians who choose to immigrate to the United Kingdom. For those I've met and interviewed from Commonwealth countries, the decision to leave is rarely made lightly. It's a family affair, often involving great sacrifices to enable one member to make the journey. These families invest heavily in their children, siblings, nieces, and nephews – funding their education, arranging marriages, or even financing their enlistment in the British Armed Forces. However, this investment comes with an unspoken agreement. Those who leave are expected to become a lifeline for those left behind, using their hard-earned British pounds to elevate their families from poverty. It's a heavy responsibility, but one that's shouldered with determination and pride. Despite the scarcity of money in these Commonwealth communities, there's an abundance of Ghanaian culture, heritage, and a certain beautiful chaos that defines their existence. And like so many others, they all nurture a dream – sometimes spoken, often unspoken – of one day returning to the land of their birth, to the villages where the scent of fermented corn and fried onions still wafts through the air on lazy Sunday mornings.

Africans from the British Army were very different compared to those from the South Pacific, Caribbean, South Asia and the Ghurkas. That's because of the linkage with the British Empire. I have always been very comfortable with my African brothers, and that's because we also have Afro-Mauritians in Mauritius who came from Mozambique and Madagascar. Africans have served in the British Army for a very long time. It's difficult to pinpoint an exact date but there's evidence of Africans serving as early as the 18th century,

During World War 1, over one million Africans served in the British Army and its colonial forces across Africa. This included soldiers from Nigeria, Gold Coast (Ghana), Sierra Leone, Gambia, and other British colonies who helped defend their territories and fight against the Germans in Africa.

Nearly one million Africans were recruited into the British Army across the African colonies in World War 2. Around 15,000 African soldiers from British colonies were killed during the War. Many others served as labourers, porters, and support staff vital to the war effort. The British colonial Army in West Africa, known as the Royal West African Frontier Force, heavily depended on locally recruited African soldiers. This force became Britain's largest colonial army in Sub-Saharan Africa during the late 19th and early 20th centuries. African soldiers faced significant racial discrimination and inequalities within the British Army during the colonial era. They were barred from reaching higher ranks, received lower pay and gratuities compared to White soldiers, and were subjected to harsh disciplinary measures like flogging. Despite their sacrifices, many African veterans of World War 2 faced neglect and a lack of proper compensation from the British Government after the War. Some African veterans and their families have been continuously seeking recognition and reparations.

Take Kenya, for example, in East Africa. During World War 1 and World War 2, thousands of Kenyans were recruited into the British colonial forces known as the King's African Rifles (KAR). They served in various African campaigns and significantly contributed to the war efforts. After Kenya gained independence in 1963, the British Army established the British Army Training Unit Kenya (BATUK) in 1964. This permanent training facility near Nanyuki allows British troops to conduct exercises and training in Kenya under an agreement with the Kenyan government. Despite the controversies, the British Army maintains a presence in Kenya through BATUK, conducting training exercises and supporting civil engineering and medical projects for local populations. The Kenyan government has allowed this arrangement to continue, likely due to the economic benefits it brings.

Here in the UK, I have the pleasure of knowing thousands of African brothers from Ghana, Nigeria, Zimbabwe, Malawi, Gambia, Uganda, South Africa, Ivory Coast, and many others still in the ranks. However, one incident comes to mind when I realised that Commonwealth veterans were still facing challenges in the UK. I remember getting an email from an organisation concerning a Commonwealth veteran sleeping in his car in the North East. He had lost his house and the council wouldn't support him as he was not British – the cost of becoming a British national is not affordable for everyone, and we will discuss this later. The local council would not consider that he had served for seven years in the British Army. After talking with this organisation trying to support this Commonwealth veteran, we found out which regiment he served with and tried to see if they would support one of their own. This was more difficult than I thought. The British Army has 70 corps and regimental badges, which makes it like a football team to which each person belongs. You might believe that each of those corps and regiments would support their people after the military, but that's not always the case. I am lucky that the Royal Regiment of Fusiliers, my first corps regiment, has a motto that says: Once a Fusilier, always a Fusilier. And they live up to it. I still actively engage with the regiment and represent the South West. I get regular invitations to the corps regimental parade, and the RRF, in many ways, are model regiments that one day others will follow. Returning to the young Ghanaian veteran, I am still waiting to hear back from the supporting organisation. I do, however, know that the RBL has been involved and offered him £150 and a blanket (as this was in the winter of 2023).

Winter 2023 also saw the loss of a Commonwealth veteran from Ghana, Bernard Amoah, who served in 17 Port and Maritime Regiment, (a regiment of the British Army's Royal Logistics Corps). He suddenly lost his life due to a gardening accident at his new home; he had just transitioned from the British military six months earlier. This was another sad and challenging time. I remember meeting him and his colleagues at the Commemoration Parade for the Black, Business, Art and Music Festival in Southampton in October, and this tragedy took place a month later. This was his first appearance after he decided to terminate his 11 years of service in the Army. One day, jokingly, I said to him: "You look very civilian with your hair and beard." He laughed. I didn't get to converse further as this was a busy day. But when I heard the family needed help with the funeral, I was able to do my very best to support his wife and his brother, who was also serving in the US. On a sombre autumn day, I found myself driving to the church with Abdoulie, the Chair of The United Voice of African Association (TUVAA). The air in the car was heavy with the weight of our shared sorrow as we discussed the untimely funeral we were about to attend. Our hearts ached for the young man who had left behind a grieving wife and children far too soon.

As we navigated the streets of Southampton, I couldn't help but reflect on Abdoulie's remarkable journey. A native of Gambia, he had become a pillar of the African community in our city, tirelessly working to amplify the voices of his fellow Commonwealth people through TUVAA. I recalled how he had reached out to me last year, seeking collaboration to represent black Africans and Commonwealth members serving in the Armed Forces. Our conversation drifted to happier memories, particularly the resounding success of TUVAA's recent endeavours. On 1 October, marking the beginning of Black History Month in the UK, Abdoulie and his team had orchestrated a groundbreaking event – the first Black festival in the South East and South West regions. The celebration had drawn an impressive crowd of over 4,000 attendees, a testament to the community's hunger for representation and cultural recognition. As we pulled into the church car park, I marvelled at Abdoulie's ability to balance the joys of cultural celebration with the solemn duties of supporting community members in times of loss. His dedication to fostering unity and providing a voice for Africans in Southampton shone through in both moments of triumph and sorrow. Stepping out of the car, we straightened our attire and shared a moment of silent understanding. Today, we would stand together to honour a life cut short, while also celebrating the strength and resilience of our diverse community. With heavy hearts but unwavering resolve, we made our way into the church, ready to offer comfort and support to those who needed it most.

Chapter Four

The Forgotten South Asian Veterans

The legacy of South Asians fighting for Britain goes as far back as the early 18th and 19th centuries, with the "Jewel in the Crown" for many people being India. British India comprised the entire sub-continent, including the territory now found in Pakistan and Bangladesh, and was known as the Indian Empire. It was not a homogeneous country, either in terms of race, religion or politics. British India contained people of the Muslim, Sikh, Hindu, Christian and Buddhist faiths. The many races extended from the Garhwali from the foothills of the Himalaya mountains to the Tamils from the south of India.

The formal establishment of an Indian army which included Indian soldiers occurred in 1895 when the Government of India raised the first army, officially called the Indian Army. The East India Company expanded its control over the Indian subcontinent. The first purely Indian troops used by the British were watchmen employed in each of the presidencies of the British East India Company to protect their trading stations. Later, as Britain expanded its presence in India, a new structure was formed to group Indian troops into four commands: Bengal, Madras (including Burma), Bombay (including Sind, Quetta, and Aden), and the Punjab (including the North-West Frontier and the Punjab Frontier Force). By the early 19th century, the Company's army was 250,000-strong, larger than that of many nations. The officers were British and there were several regiments composed only of Europeans. But the vast majority of Company soldiers were Indian.

It was on 21 October 1914 that the Indian soldiers were sent to the frontline in the hope that they could at least delay the German push for Calais. These brave men were merely an advance guard for what would become a colossal army, providing 1.4 million men to the Allied war effort, which was more than Scotland, Wales and Ireland combined. Most were convinced by posters in Hindi and Urdu that would say: 'Easy life, lots of respect, very little danger, good pay'! Only 10% of these men served in Europe; 90% were sent to warmer battlefields in Gallipoli, Salonika, the East and the Middle East to protect the Persian and Iraqi oil fields which were vital for the British troops. This came at a cost of 53,000 Indians who gave their lives, another 64,000 were wounded and nearly 4,000 were taken prisoner. Twelve of them were awarded the Victoria Cross which are not easily won even nowadays. These courageous men thought they were serving, fighting, suffering and dying as equals under the flag but the fact was that Indian soldiers were underpaid; they received about a quarter of the wage of a British soldier. However, they were all well looked after during their time in Britain. From 1914 to 1916, wounded Indian soldiers from the Western Front were brought to Britain for treatment. Special hospitals were set up along the South Coast in Brighton, Bournemouth and Brockenhurst. There were also convalescent camps at Milford on Sea and Barton. In Brighton, the Royal Pavilion was converted into a hospital, with further hospitals in York Place and the Old Workhouse. For those soldiers who died, there were crematoria for Hindus and Sikhs, and a burial ground in Woking for Muslim soldiers. In the hospitals, great care was taken to accommodate the various religious requirements of the soldiers. In the Royal Pavilion and Dome Hospital there were nine separate kitchens to cater for different dietary needs. Tents were put up in the grounds for religious worship. Opportunities for recreational pursuits were provided including outings to London to see the sights. King George V and Queen Mary visited the Pavilion on several occasions, presenting soldiers with bravery awards, including six Victoria Crosses. Though the soldiers were all well looked after, interaction with local people was not encouraged. Precautions were taken to keep the soldiers confined to the hospital grounds; some soldiers felt like prisoners and complained, but to no avail.

(https://www.exploringsurreyspast.org.uk/themes/subjects/military/india-woking/indian-soldiers-in-britain/)

Things changed rapidly after victory was declared and the troops took off their uniforms. One source stated that since there were 11,000 British soldiers also in transition, they had priority over jobs. People would say, 'They must come first.' Even though the Indians have served in the army and had medals to prove it, they were heavily discriminated against. The *Brighton Herald* reported that the town's public had been 'agog' to see the these 'warriors from the East' march through Brighton but were disappointed by the discreet manner in which they were admitted to the hospitals; in Cardiff they were called the Black 'colony'; in Liverpool 'the coloured' men were branded as the aggressors in most disputes. On 23 June 1919, Lord Milner wrote a "Memorandum on the Repatriation of Coloured Men" where Indians, Blacks and Chinese were offered free repatriation tickets, a five pounds golden handshake and a couple of pounds of travel expenses. The *SS Kurmansk* left Cardiff with only 63 Indians and 50 Adenese, while *SS Santille* left for Jamaica with 147 Soldiers. Every effort possible was made to make these soldiers want to return, but most had wives and children and had started to adapt to their British lives. From this time, different prejudices have morphed into policy – all process, no principles. I'll dive deeper into this in Part Two.

During the writing of this book, I was caught by the magnificent D-Day 80 Commemoration in Portsmouth and got to know the story of Warrant Officer Subadar Sain Khan, a Pakistani paratrooper and paratrooper on D-Day. His own grandson, Razal Mustafa, who is a British born, was not aware of his service. It was only when he went to Pakistan and saw his medals that he was very proud to know his grandfather served with the British Army.
(https://www.shotstv.com/watch/vod/52473555).

Although I have not personally served with many South Indians during my time, every effort was made during their time in Britain to accommodate their various dietary, religious and cultural needs – since then, Sikhs are allowed to wear turbans rather than helmets and berets. The primary focus of the British Armed Forces today, especially the British Army, is to build leaders. Anyone who has done a few years in the service will have gained extensive leadership knowledge which I have elaborated in both my previous books. As a career strategist, I have worked with hundreds of service leavers and carefully observed the career path of thousands of service leavers in the marketplace. Underneath it all is the ability to belong – this, unfortunately, is not a science but a need that was first highlighted by the famous Abraham Maslow just after WW1 with his famous pyramid of the hierarchy of needs. The need for love and belonging sits right in the middle – between physiological needs, safety and security, and love and self-esteem and self-actualisation. According to the Census of 2021, more than 100,000 foreign and Commonwealth veterans live in the UK, with another 10,000 still serving in the Armed Forces today. So why is belonging essential for us, and how can units, garrisons, and commanders make foreign and Commonwealth individuals feel more a part of an organisation?

In his latest book, 'Be Useful' author, actor and athlete Arnold Schwarzenegger talks about how he wanted to not just fit in to American society but belong to this nation. At that time, people didn't know what a bodybuilder was and journalists would write about this as an art rather than as a sport. So, Arnold made it his mission to tell everyone what bodybuilding was. He left his birth country, Austria, at the age of 21 for the American dream. He knew the American way of life would not be easy after living in a communist country from a young age – in a one-bedroom home in Thal, a village just west of Graz which is the second biggest city after Vienna. His first dream from a young age was to be a star. In his Netflix docuseries, 'Arnold', he spoke about his dream of a life as a bodybuilder, starring in movies and making millions of dollars. It was when he saw a picture of Reg Park featured on the poster of 'Hercules' in 1961 that he realised what had been done and what could be done. This clearly indicates that Arnold Schwarzenegger's incredible story from bodybuilder to Hollywood actor to American politician all began in Thal – he clearly had a dream, a vision and a plan. Like Arnold, thousands of Commonwealth, Gurkhas and British overseas personnel moved to the UK for a reason. Whether this move was driven by a dream for a better life, a vision of prosperity or a plan to improve themselves, everyone who enlisted in the British Armed Forces joined because they wanted to be connected and achieve something that was perhaps impossible back in their home countries. Their resilience and determination are truly admirable.

My point here is that every member of the Armed Forces needs to feel a part of and belong to the broader British society during and after their service and to tell the world about their career – especially for Gurkhas and Commonwealth personnel who joined the Armed Forces and were prepared to lay down their lives in serving to the highest authority of this country. However, the experience you will read in the following chapters may sometimes be very different. Even Arnold, who already had great potential when he arrived in the US in 1968, quickly realised that bodybuilding was not seen as a sport but more of an art. Because of his strong Austrian accent, he too was looked at as a 'Bloody Foreigner' although no one had the audacity to challenge him physically. Every reporter would describe him as an artist rather than an athlete, unlike today. So, to achieve his dream, he changed the perception of the American people by building a community and educating society about the sport. Similarly, Gurkhas and other foreign and Commonwealth veterans face unique challenges and experiences that are often misunderstood, but they too strive to change perceptions and build a sense of belonging.

The largest number of South Asians serving in the UK come from Nepal. This is because the British Indian Army, also referred to as the Indian Army under British rule, was a significant military force that served the British Empire until India's independence in 1947. Then, we also have the Gurkhas from Nepal. Looking back to how far the Gurkhas served alongside the British Armed Forces, we can see approximately 200 years – from 1814 to 1816, during the Anglo–Nepal war, the British saw their combat skills displayed. Consequently, after the peace treaty was signed, negotiations commenced to formally incorporate Gurkha soldiers into the British East India Company's army. I have personally served and known many "Gurkhas" – a name the Nepalese soldiers earned from the British due to their association with the hill town in central Nepal, Gorkha region of Nepal, during their time in the British Army. In my conversation with Prem (not his real name), who is a retired Gurkha in Rushmoor, he reminded me of the story of the Gurkhas, which at the beginning was just about joining forces and being respected for who they are. He talked about how many Nepalese were able to improve their family lives while serving in the UK, and many had no dream of a life in the UK.

For this reason, many loyalists came to the UK, fought for decades alongside the British Army, and then returned home. I remember Captain Morgan from the Parachute Regiment during my training with the Royal Regiment of Fusiliers in Litchfield near Birmingham saying: 'If you are at war and you have a Royal Marine, a paratrooper and a Gurkha next to you, it means you are in good company.' And he was damn right. But Raj also reminded me of the disloyalty he faced as he looked at his army pension in 1983, in contrast to a British-born or even another Commonwealth veteran who joined during a similar time. The Gurkha pension scheme was designed to provide a rate suitable for retirement in Nepal, as Gurkhas traditionally would return after their service. It was based on the lowest cost of living compared to the UK, as some were also based in Hong Kong around 1997. We also had the Tripartite Agreement between Britain, India, and Nepal, which made the issue more complex in 1974. However, as more Gurkha veterans chose to make Britain their home country after retirement, Prem and the rest of the Gurkha community are campaigning today that their pension should equal that of British soldiers since they face the exact same living costs. Gurkhas have been loyal soldiers to Britain for over 200 years, dating to 1816 when the mighty British East India Company found itself locked in a fierce struggle with the warriors of Nepal's Kingdom. Although the British emerged victorious, they had been so impressed by the Gurkhas' martial prowess that they decided to make them allies instead of enemies. In 1816, the Treaty of Sagauli was signed, and around 5,000 Gurkha soldiers were recruited into the East India Company's armies. This marked the beginning of a lasting military brotherhood between the Gurkhas and British forces that continues until today. When the guns of the First World War began to thunder across Europe, the legendary Gurkha warriors answered the call to arms, making significant contributions and sacrifices that deserve our appreciation and recognition.

Over 200,000 of these fearless fighters from Nepal rallied to the British cause, leaving their mountain homes to brave the horrors of trench warfare. From the blood-soaked beaches of Gallipoli to the blistering deserts of Palestine and Egypt, the Gurkhas' reputation for unbreakable resolve and ferocity in battle grew with each campaign. But such valour came at a terrible cost – by the War's end, a staggering 20,000 Gurkha lives had been sacrificed. Their extraordinary courage was recognised with the highest military honour: the Victoria Cross. Though this ultimate accolade was not extended to Gurkha troops until 1911, 26 of these sons of Nepal have etched their names in history as recipients of the prized medal.

In the shadow of the Himalayas, Nepal has stood proud and sovereign for centuries. Its people, known for their bravery and resilience, have long embodied the spirit of "Be useful" – a motto that still resonates with everyone today. Among these stalwart Nepalis are the Gurkhas, soldiers whose courage and loyalty have become legendary in the British Army. The story of the Gurkhas is one of valour, but also of inequality. As time passed, the Gurkhas became an integral part of the British military, fighting in numerous conflicts across the globe. However, despite their unwavering service, a disparity in treatment emerged. In 2023, a group of Gurkha veterans, under the banner of the British Gurkha Satyagraha Joint Committee, penned a poignant letter to then-Prime Minister Rishi Sunak. Their words echoed the frustration of decades, highlighting a stark inequality in pension rights between Gurkha veterans and their British counterparts. The letter brought to light a pivotal moment in 2007 when the British Government implemented the Gurkha Offer to Transfer (GOTT). This initiative allowed Gurkhas who had served after 1 July 1997, to transfer their service from the Gurkha Pension Scheme to the more favourable Armed Forces Pension Scheme. It was a step towards equality, but one that left many behind. For those who had retired before 1997, the changes brought little comfort. These veterans, numbering around 8,000, continued to receive pensions based on a lower threshold – a remnant of historical policies designed for retirement in Nepal rather than the UK. The disparity was stark, with some Gurkha veterans receiving pensions up to 300% lower than their British counterparts. The veterans' letter to Sunak was more than a plea; it was a reminder of a promise made. They recalled a meeting in September 2021 with Ben Wallace, then Secretary of State for Defence, who had encouraged them to include every issue in their negotiations. Yet, as the letter pointed out, subsequent talks seemed to sideline the crucial issue of equal pensions. As the story unfolds, the Gurkhas' fight for equality continues. Their campaign, rooted in a rich history of service and sacrifice, challenges the notion of fairness in a modern world. It's a tale that intertwines the sovereign pride of Nepal with the complex dynamics of international military service, reminding us that the echoes of historical decisions can resonate long into the present, affecting lives and legacies across continents.

(https://kathmandupost.com/national/2023/04/04/gurkha-veterans-memo-uk-pm-sunak-seeking-redressal-of-their-pension-issues)

Chapter Five

The Forgotten South Pacific Veterans

As an islander myself, I took great interest in understanding the perspective of Fijians. To first understand its people you need to understand its cultures – something I am progressively learning. Fiji is an archipelago consisting of more than 330 islands, of which about 110 are permanently inhabited. The total land area of Fiji is approximately 18,300 square kilometres (7,100 sq. mi), the two major islands – Viti Levu and Vanua Levu – accounting for 87% of the total lands. Other main islands are Taveuni, Kadavu, Rabi, Vatulele, Beqa, and Qamea. In addition, there are several important groups of islands: Rotuma (8 islands), Lau (57), Moala part of the Lau group (3), Lomaiviti (12), Mamanuca (10), and the Yasawa group (20). Those 110 islands are then divided into 15 provinces, 195 districts, and 1,193 villages inhabited by a happy race of Fijians from Melanesia, Polynesia, India, China and other nationalities. Fiji has a really interesting system when it comes to leadership. Imagine the country divided into 14 different areas called provinces. Now, each of these provinces has its own big boss, similar to a local king, called a paramount chief. These chiefs are super important – they're like the traditional leaders that people look up to. Here's the cool part: in 13 out of the 14 provinces, there's one main chief who's in charge. But there's this one rebel province called Kadavu that does things a bit differently. Instead of having just one big chief, they've got nine! Each of these nine chiefs is the top dog in their own little area. These chiefs aren't just for show either. People in each province actually turn to them for advice on all sorts of important matters, such as family rights and how to take care of their homeland. It's like having a wise grandparent for an entire community! To keep everything running smoothly between these traditional leaders and the modern government, there's a special ministry that acts like a bridge between the two. Pretty neat system, right?

I started this book by talking about Livai, a Fijian brother who left us way too early and whom I never had the opportunity to know until I met with his family and children at his funeral. Fijians have been loyal soldiers in the British Army going back as far as 1919. The first person to attempt to join the British army was Josefa Lalabalavu Vana'ali'ali Sukuna born on 22 April 1888 on the island of Viti Levu. He was studying at the University of Oxford in 1914 when WW1 broke out and was keen to see battle. However this Fijian student was Black and was rejected by the British authorities who refused to enlist non-Whites; he joined the French Foreign Legion and won a Croix de Guerre.

Ratu Josefa was wounded in late 1915 and returned to Fiji. Ratu Josefa then tried unsuccessfully to enlist in the New Zealand Pioneer Battalion. It was spring 1915, the Prince and his Legionnaires were in the trenches in Berthonval with the First Brigade of the Moroccan Division, part of the 2nd Infantry Regiment of the 1st Foreign Legion company. Sukuna mounted an assault on the "Ouvrages Blancs" near Neuville-Saint-Vaast on 9 May 1915. Carency and Souchez followed, with their scenes of blood and fury, where the Fijian was to receive his first Citation for Acts of Bravery.

In September 1915, Sukuna took part in the Battle of Champagne and on the 28th, in Souain, he was wounded in the temple and hospitalised in Lyon. "I am conscious of doing my duty," he wrote to his family, "but war is hell. The sight of blood makes me nauseous and the effect of the conflict on the local population brings tears to my eyes."

In January 1916, the British authorities who were ruling Fiji at the time urged him to return to his homeland. He disembarked in Suva on 30 March, his head swathed in bandages. As a native islander subject to the decisions of the colonial authorities, Sukuna became a civil servant and tried to convince the British to send Fijians to the front. He was to return to France in May 1917, not as a soldier but as a sergeant and worker in the Fiji Labour Corps. In Calais, Sukuna and 100 other men worked at the port. In January 1918, they were sent to Marseille and from there to Taranto in Italy. Eleven of his co-workers died in France and were buried in either Calais, Marseille or Taranto.

In September 1918, the Fiji Labour Corps set sail for the Pacific. After a short period as a barrister at the London Bar, this Fijian "to the core" became a leading politician in the islands. During the Second World War, he exhorted Fijians "to spill their blood for Great Britain": 2,000 fought alongside the Allies. During Fiji's decolonisation process, Ratu Sukuna was president of the legislative council.

The "Father of modern Fijians" retired in April 1958 and died on 30 May on board a ship taking him to England. Henceforth, in the Fijian islands, the last Monday in May became a public holiday known as Ratu Sukuna Day. Fiji: a Pacific idyll home to rugby and a hero of the Great War. (https://www.history-pas-de-calais.com/first-world-war/they-came-from-across-the-globe/fijians/)

It is the stories about Ratu Josefa that have become a motivation for the thousands of Fijians serving in our Armed Forces today. Livai Boila was one of them. Livai was bored of his islander life and had been moping: after all, he was jobless, homeless and loveless – he did not know which one was worse. But now it dawned on him that he could find a new sense of purpose worth all the rigours and risks of serving in the Army by stepping into the legacy of his ancestors. He would have a new career and a new home with a new family of brothers in which to belong.

He came to the UK from his Island in Fiji with his close family friend John. Life in the British Army can be unique for everyone, just as life after the Army is also uniquely challenging and very personal for everyone. Livai, alongside his friend, came to the UK and joined the

Royal Highlander Fusiliers in Scotland until he was discharged by the Army and had to do cash-in-hand work around Scotland to survive. I have been to Scotland many times and now we run our academy in partnership with a few Scottish universities. From my viewpoint, the Scottish can be much more accommodating to the Commonwealth, but the Home Office still directs them at No 10, which means their immigration rules are similar to England and Wales. Unfortunately, Livai was never given the correct information on his immigration status after leaving the military. People like myself, and those from foreign and Commonwealth backgrounds, are given an exemption on their immigration status for the duration of their time in uniform (see 'A Cry for Belonging'). This is the most complex system in the history of the people movement and, in many ways, a capitalised tool for many political parties, as explained in Part One of this book.

Back in the year 2016, when Livai was really struggling to make ends meet, he then reached out to his blood brother John, who I had the honour to serve with at 17 Port & Maritime Regiment in Marchwood, Southampton, during my time as a Movement Controller in the British Army. John tried his best to get his blood brother back on his feet; he trained him daily, went for a run, got him back into the gym so that he could rejoin the British Army. After a few weeks, they both went to the Army Careers Centre in Southampton to enlist him back in the Army. This was five years after he was discharged – going back in after a period of struggle on Civvy Street is fairly standard for most Commonwealth and even UK-born soldiers. I have covered this transition stage in my third book, Reinvented – Leavers to Leaders in Practise. However, for John and Livai, it was then that John realised that Livai had never applied for his indefinite leave to remain. In those days it was (and still is) the soldier's responsibility to gain legal rights after the military. Many of my UK connections think that because we wear uniforms and serve this country, we should automatically have the legal right to live in the

UK. This is far from the truth. I had my own my personal challenges with immigration with the Home Office, and if you are reading this book, it is likely you had your own challenges or know someone who has. Unfortunately, the Home Office and the British Armed Forces do not talk to each other: this is why as you see stories such as that of Andrew Williams in Chapter Eight. He was made illegal based on these same facts and was impoverished by the system and lived for five years without access to NHS and dental treatment. This was in 2013.

Livai's passport was taken away from him by the Career's Office and he was sent to Immigration in 2017 – did they have the right to do this? He had to report to the local police every week, and on one occasion, he was locked away in a cell overnight for questioning at the Bitterne Police Station in Southampton after he had to live illegally in the UK, unable to work and get support for three years. These are questions that need answering. Today, the British Army is labelling foreign and Commonwealth citizens as 'Non-UK' and has created General Administrative Instruction (AGAI 59) as a rule to make every soldier understand their responsibility for immigration after leaving the forces. This process is not morally unethical, but it is without principles. The British have a moral right to support its service personnel, but now that the Commonwealth and those from Nepal and other British Overseas Territories are defined as 'Non-UK', I wonder what the future holds. I will cover this in more detail in Part Three of this book. We have all witnessed many other experiences of Fijian veterans who were wrongly advised and not rightly supported after their time in the military. I know many left the UK in desperation because this was their only way out.

So, Livai's application for indefinite leave to remain was a long, struggling process. Luckily for him, John knew someone at Associated British Ports Southampton (ABP), where Livai was able to work as a driver for the Isle of Wright Ferry full-time until he passed away during an accident in 2023. I remember seeing John in tears at the funeral; I knew John as this robust Fijian rugby player and a very skilled Kalmar Operator during our time at the container park and working in the Falklands Shed in 17 Port and Maritime Regiment in Marchwood. Seeing him made me cry and I realised the pain he must be going through. From my experience of working with many Commonwealth veterans in the UK, I see that many are still playing to avoid losing when they should be playing to win. This is the difference between surviving and thriving. Unfortunately, this is easier said than done. The system that those guys found themselves under has been designed to push them beyond just surviving. In 2023, the House of Lords published an excellent research briefing on 'Support for Veterans'. This is the first time a report has been compiled; however, when I read the table of contents, I could not see a chapter on foreign and Commonwealth veterans. Further reading led me to realise they were not aware of this community living in the UK. Was it written assuming that all UK veterans are equal or have equal rights? To me, it brings to mind the story of a monkey, a tiger, and an elephant being asked to demonstrate their intelligence by climbing a tree. Totally unfair some may think, but that's the rule.

Similarly, I have come across Commonwealth veterans who were discharged within weeks of being drug-tested positive in the Armed Forces. James (not his real name to protect his identity), who served for 12 years, tested positive and was eventually kicked out of the Army. The British Army has no tolerance for reckless behaviour and I totally agree with this protocol. The Values and Standards of the British Army apply to everyone, regardless of rank or status. However, James was so ashamed of the sudden consequences to his career that he never applied for his indefinite leave to remain. Although his discharge from the Army would have no consequences on his right to leave and stay in the UK or even become a British citizen, he found himself unable to work when the Home Office introduced a Biometric Residency Permit (BRP).

James was forced to go into the dead ground (the lowest level in society) with no right to work, no right to leave, and no access to NHS or Welfare. James stayed in the dead ground for ten years until recently, when he applied for his ILR. I am not debating his actions prior to being tested drug positive, but I am questioning if something could have been done to someone who served 12 years for the Country and had the right to stay. We all know someone at work who is on medical drugs for wellbeing. If James were a UK citizen, then this would not be such an issue, as being tested positive is not a crime for a civilian. Should the British Army be more tolerant? No: it wouldn't be a functional Army if it were. However, I also believe that due welfare should be in place to allow this individual to transition as a civilian – after all, he served for 12 years to protect the interests of the UK. This reminds me of a famous line from George Orwell's book 'Animal Farm': "All animals are equal, but some animals are equal to others." Rules are rules, but one needs to assess the impact on those who are less fortunate. James was kicked out of the British Army within days, regardless of where he was going to live and stay. For Commonwealth soldiers, this is a harsh reality, but I thank God, after ten years of hardship as an illegal immigrant British soldier, James is now living happily with his wife and children.

PART TWO
The Hostile Environments in Britain

In my attempt to showcase the historical link between Commonwealth citizens who gave their service to Britain, I came across three waves of generations. First, the post-colonial wave from the late 1940s until 1960s, mainly with Caribbeans, Africans and South Asians. A second wave from 1962 to 1990s was mostly for families and children from the first wave. However, the largest generation so far has been from 1998 to 2013 which historically has been the busiest time for Britain since WW2.

In writing this chapter, I will stretch a bit further to 1919. The Dominion, or new Commonwealth as they came to be known, played a significant part in helping Britain and its Empire emerge victoriously from two wars at a cost of about 150,000 Dominions dead in WW1 and 90,000 in WW2. As the writer and historian of immigration Randall Hansen puts it:

'The old Dominion were central to the United Kingdom's economic and foreign policy; they contributed to its international prestige and influence; and they ensured the flourishing of the English language and British culture in the international arena.' (Randall Hansen, 'Citizenship and immigration in Post-War Britain', Oxford University Press, 2000, p.17). All of this at a huge cost of lives lost during battles as we can see.

Back in 1919, politicians tried and failed in getting Indians, Africans, Chinese and Caribbeans to voluntarily leave Britain – even though they made sure to give them plenty of incentives. It was during that time that the grey area could have started to form in Britain when it comes to 'foreigners. In this chapter we will elaborate on the seven distinguishable 'hostile environments' directly affecting the livelihood of Commonwealth individuals after giving their military service. The word hostile was first used in the House of Commons when Paul Sweeney MP for Glasgow spoke about the history of life and challenges of Commonwealth veterans and Gurkhas, including the Hong Kong veterans, who served Britain. To fully understand this, we need to rewind to 1919.

In his book 'Bloody Foreigners – The Story of Immigration in Britain', Robert Winder details the calculated effort made to remove people who served from Africa, Caribbean and India. As the author describes, inch by inch, prejudices turned into policy protected by booklets, photos, lists, stamps and politics. By 1925, the Government came out with a special restriction called the Coloured Alien Seamen Order, ordering all non-Britons to register with the local police. It was then that the term 'alien' started to be used for 'non-domiciled' migrants. Today, soldiers recruited from Commonwealth countries are labelled as 'Non-UK' personnel and veterans, something that I am currently campaigning to put a stop to, since this has a negative and divisive impact for integration and the feeling of belonging, which we will talk about in Chapter Three of this book. In 1931, the Government restricted passports to only those individuals who had an existing employment offer in place and offered subsidies to firms who would employ 'British' (that is, White) seamen. But it was cheaper to employ a colonial instead of getting paid the subsidy for a 'White British' which gave life to the movement for Indian rights in Britain.

Chapter Six

The Right of Passage

Until 2023, the British Armed Forces had never paid much attention to what happened after someone was discharged from the military as a Commonwealth individual. Shockingly, in my 23 years of being engaged with the forces, it is only now that the British Army has set up a Unit and team to visit Army camps regularly for a briefing on Visas and indefinite leave to remain after leaving the military. Earlier last year, I attended a conference at Tidworth Garrison Theatre in the South West by the Army Family Federation (AFF). The AFF is an independent organisation, separate from the Army itself, that serves as the voice of Army families. It provides a confidential platform where families can raise concerns, issues or grievances without revealing their identities. It allows individuals to speak up freely and get their voices heard. During a 45-minute presentation, the immigration team highlighted the 'hostile environment' that Commonwealth and Gurkhas faced after the military.

This was the time when I realised the deep meaning of the term 'hostile environment' as we will see in the lived experiences in following chapters. But it goes further than that: everyone seemed to forget that everybody who gave their service to Britain paid for a unique '*Right of Passage*'. What do I mean by that?

In previous chapters, I introduced various individuals who came to serve in the Armed Forces and as we will see later, every single one of them paid their own costs financially of passage to enlist. Even when we look at the time when Britain was on its knees and they needed the Commonwealth to win the war against Nazi Germany, those brave men and women who joined in 1944 had to pay their way to come to Britain. Has this changed? What was the price for the 'Right of Passage' then?

Winston was born in Jamaica and came to the UK at the age of 14, later joining the Royal Air Force, serving for over 29 years. According to him, the 'Right of Passage' was £12.50 when he first travelled with his parents and sister to Britain. Today, for a Commonwealth citizen to join the Armed Forces, it can cost over $5000 as explained by those who enlisted between 2001 and 2006. The latest cohort who travelled to the UK unfortunately found themselves with an additional problem – the recruitment process is extremely slow and can take more than 6 months. Some potential soldiers had to return back home penniless after this wait, in debt to their family and friends who invested in them. We know from announcements in the media that the military is going to need to recruit at least 1,350 Commonwealth individuals to maintain its strength and 337 will join via Nepal in 2024 according to the Gurkha Brigade. So, not only do these brave souls literally pay for their 'Right of Passage' to Britain, but at the end of their service they also have to pay for their right to remain in the country. A 'Double Penalty' for the giving of your service. Of course, should they have joined whilst already being in the UK, like I did, then this would not be the same unless they had to go back and reapply for entry. In this case, they would be paying three times more for the 'Right of Passage'!

Early this year, I was asked to speak to young soldiers of the Gurkhas squadron at the army welfare of NATO Allied Rapid Reaction Corps (ARRC) operating at a 3-star headquarters in Gloucestershire. This camp has about 400 people from more than 20 nations according to the British Army website.

The experience of a Gurkha's life in the UK today may not be so different to the experience of those who left during the pre-2000 era. Back in those days, after giving service, a Gurkha was expected to return to his village and retire on his mediocre army pension which was decided upon once commencing enlistment. The Gurkha had no option, a modern form of indentured servitude. As for their families, according to Raj, the wife may have obtained an indefinite leave to remain as a result of any children being born in the UK, but the soldier lost this right to remain when their service came to an end with the military. This created a horrible situation for the families because at the point the veteran had no right to remain in the UK, they had to depart back to their country of birth and reapply to join their families.

'This is one of the most horrible experiences I can imagine as a father – having to be invited by my wife to come back to a country that I have previously served,' said Pradip, who I met in Aldershot. Veteran Gurkhas had to be sponsored by their wives and if, at the point of re-entry, the wife decided she had had enough of him, then this could lead to a completely different story. I can imagine many families have suffered due to this system. Fast-forward to today: the new Gurkha has a contract of 12 years and must achieve a certain rank before he is then allowed to either renew his contract or transfer to the wider British Army. I think this new arrangement is a better option for recruits as they are also able to gain indefinite leave to remain as part of their service.

Speaking with Raj, a retired Gurkha soldier who served with distinction for 20 years in the British Army, he longed to be reunited with his wife and children who unfortunately were not allowed to accompany him. He now lives in a small flat in Southampton, far from his family in Nepal.

Raj served in some of the most dangerous conflicts, risking his life for the UK. However, when he tried to bring his family to join him after his retirement, his application got stuck in the complex visa process. He couldn't meet the high-income threshold required to sponsor their visas, despite having a modest but steady income as a door supervisor. The separation had been incredibly difficult for Raj, at times affecting his mental wellbeing. Being a door supervisor did not help either: he had lost all his honour and people treated him like another immigrant on the door. He missed his family dearly and worried about their wellbeing in Nepal. The long wait for a visa decision had added to his stress. By the time his family were granted their visa, his wife decided to file for a divorce and to this day, Raj has never been able to meet his children who were born while he was serving.

It was only in 2009, that the UK Government introduced new policies to recognise the unique service of Gurkhas in the British Army's Brigade of Gurkhas. These policies allowed Gurkhas who retired before 1 July 1997, and their families, to settle in the UK. Many of these brave soldiers have suffered silently around the issue of visas and indefinite leave to remain. Talking about this experience for many has become almost a taboo subject as it brings back so many bad memories. No wonder that today, after 212 years serving the Crown, very few offspring of the Gurkhas have chosen to join the British Army Forces – it is unlikely their children will ever join when they have witnessed the treatment of their parents. This is a subject we will cover later in the next chapter.

Until lately, there has not been much information on how to prepare for life after the military. The 'Non-UK' brief I attended at ARRC was not a pleasant one and I feel hugely sorry for those whose job it is to travel from regiment to regiment and deliver those presentations. It is one of the cruellest presentations you can find yourself listening to. The closest feeling I get from listening to those briefings is the book 'Man's Search for Meaning', a 1946 memoir by Viktor Frankl, a renowned Austrian neurologist, psychiatrist, and Holocaust survivor. The book chronicles Frankl's experiences as a prisoner in Nazi concentration camps during World War 2 and outlines his psychotherapeutic method of finding meaning in life, even amidst the most horrific circumstances. Serving men and women from the Commonwealth today are reminded constantly, on every side, that they don't belong and that they are classified as 'Non-UK' and as such are politically considered differently.

I remember the feelings of resentment I felt listening to this 45-minute briefing as a veteran who had left the military 18 years ago – hearing myself referred to as Non-UK personnel and wondering how those young soldiers in the audience felt. This was the question running through my head as I turned around to look at their anxious faces. I was not surprised that after the briefing, no one asked any questions: the room was completely silent, and I could sense the low morale and crushed pride in the room. This was a difficult climate for me whilst being seated next to the speaker. It was a huge effort to wake up from the dark cloud that had descended upon the room as I realised it was my job to give those guys a feeling of hope for the future. My intention was clear: to attempt to help them figure out the Commonwealth dream, if such a dream ever existed. Unlike the American dream, the Commonwealth dream is barely imaginable.

During the writing of this book, I spoke with three different groups of veterans. The first Commonwealth wave to come to the UK were after 1948. They took the risk of travelling to the UK, paying for the right of passage for their visa entry, paying for their return flights (required by Immigration), sustaining themselves while being in the UK and applying to join the British military. The second wave was in 2003: this time the British military had become alerted by this desire for Commonwealth citizens to join the forces and started to invite people to join. The recruitment team would travel to those faraway lands and hosted huge recruitment days. After selection, the candidates would need to show proof of income to travel to the UK. The third wave is what is still ongoing today: they apply to join online, where they upload all the documentations; they need to find a sponsor (someone to pay for their living costs in Britain and take full responsibility) then buy their return flight.

The attitude towards the Commonwealth has not changed significantly from the mid-1940s to the early 2000s among historians and commentators in Britain. This was a period of significant historical shifts, marked by the end of the British Empire, the Cold War, and the rise of the non-aligned movement. During this time, there was a prevailing sense of uncertainty and ambiguity regarding the Commonwealth's nature, functions, and potential. In the late 1940s and 1950s, historians and political scientists writing about the Commonwealth expressed profound uncertainty over what it could achieve. This uncertainty did not stem from specific events like Britain's relationship with Europe, the Suez Crisis, or the rise of the non-aligned movement. Instead, the uncertainty was rooted in the fundamental question of what precisely the Commonwealth was and what kind of connections and bonds held it together. Historians like Arnold J. Toynbee and Kenneth C. Wheare described the Commonwealth as an abstraction, a nascent and unprecedented experiment whose bonds were extensive yet impossible to measure precisely. Wheare are called it a "heterogeneous thing" with an uncertain future. This sense of uncertainty persisted through the decades. In the 1960s and 1970s, commentators like D.W. Brogan and Nicholas Mansergh continued to view the Commonwealth as a work in progress, with Mansergh calling it an "unparalleled experiment." Even as late as the 1990s, after the end of the Cold War and the transition from the British Empire, historians like John Darwin portrayed the Commonwealth as an entity whose precise nature and potential remained unclear, reflecting the "experimental, tentative nature" of its existence. Rather than expressing optimism or pessimism, the prevailing sentiment among historians and commentators was one of profound ambiguity and uncertainty regarding the Commonwealth's capacity to realise its supposed latent potential rooted in the willingness of its members to work together. This uncertainty stemmed not from specific events but from the very abstraction and novelty of the Commonwealth as a concept and institution. So, while attitudes towards other aspects of the Commonwealth may have changed, the fundamental uncertainty about its nature and future prospects persisted from the 1940s through to the early 2000s among historians and intellectuals in Britain.

During my research for this book, I came across a brilliant work on immigration to Britain by Robert Winder titled *'Bloody Foreigners'*. Winder discusses how the comprehensive role of migrants has been largely omitted from the national narrative. He states, "Time and again I came across delineations of the national character which failed to view it as a product of a cosmopolitan ancestry." The rest of the book provides a compelling account of the crucial role foreigners have played in the history of this country. Each new wave of immigrants has helped to reshape and reinvent Britain, almost always for the better. However, the experiences and contributions of these foreigners – whether they were French Jews living in York in the 12th century, Italian musicians and even Africans who brought vibrancy to the Elizabethan era, or the West Indians whose labour was crucial in the post-War reconstruction – were rarely documented or discussed in Britain.

Today, a Commonwealth veteran and his family are treated in the same category as the illegal immigrant who came off the boat yesterday, a term that has been used repetitively. Every country has a right, even a duty, to choose who should come in and who should be asked to leave. But there is a difference between those who come to give their service and are ready to sacrifice everything in the process and those who come to ask for help and refuge. The economy is simple: one adds value by paying their Tax and National Insurance, whereas the other does not. Dr Krish Kandiah OBE, the founder of the Sanctuary Foundation, a charity that supports refugees from Ukraine, Afghanistan and other countries, said in a recent interview that we have to differentiate between the different types of immigration. There are those who come to thrive and contribute such as a doctor or a nurse in the NHS, on which the UK is highly dependent to help the country be the wonderful safe place it is. The second type of migrant is the humanitarian migrant who is not here to earn a living or get a job but to flee war, persecution, catastrophe and crisis. I think we need to add a third category, which I think Krish would definitely agree with: our Commonwealth soldiers who come to serve this country. I said earlier that Britain has no idea of the global recruitment effort for the Commonwealth to join the Armed Forces. Perhaps we should also look at the contribution they made in the 24 years of service they gave to Britain and aim to fully understand the right of passage that they paid and the right to remain which they all have to pay.

Chapter Seven

Visa and Indefinite Leave to Remain

'What must we do to be treated fairly in this country?' These were the words from Iveri during our conversation about his time in the Rifles.

We know that many Commonwealth soldiers have been struggling with settlement in the UK since 1948. In her novel *'Small Island'*, Andrea Levy tells the story of Jamaican immigrants in Britain after World War 2 through the perspectives of four narrators: Hortense and Gilbert, a Jamaican couple, and Queenie and Bernard, a White English couple. The novel explores the experiences of Caribbean immigrants in post-war Britain, dealing with themes of racism, identity, belonging and starting anew in the "mother country." The terminology 'Coloured' is constantly used to describe a person who is non-White. In one chapter, they would be asking: how coloured were the people? I suppose in those days, you were either White or non-White. In its 'Inclusive Britain' strategy published on 17 March 2022, the UK Government stated it "will no longer use the term 'BAME' to refer to different ethnic minority groups within society." This decision was made to "communicate more effectively on racial issues and to avoid lumping together different ethnic minority groups" with diverse perspectives and experiences. This move followed the Commission on Race and Ethnic Disparities report in March 2021 which found that aggregate terms like 'BAME' were "no longer helpful and should be dropped" in favour of focusing on understanding disparities for specific ethnic groups.

On two occasions, I was called a person of colour just recently. The first one was by a reporter who wanted to know my racial background over the phone and naively asked me if I was a person of colour. He is a very respectful guy who himself comes from an Asian background and did not offend me one bit. However, on that same day, I walked into Portsmouth University and while talking with the recruitment lady, I wanted to know how the university would describe people of a different racial background. She announced to me that they now use the term 'people of global majority'. I found this new label fascinating – perhaps it means that Commonwealth citizens and anyone who comes from a different racial background are actually a majority outside the UK. The Commonwealth is made up of 56 countries in 2024, including Africa, which according to statistictime.com results has a projected population of around 1.49 billion (or 1,494,993,924) people. If you head to countrymetres.info/en/india, you will be able to see the live status of the population of India which is increasing every second from 1.45 billion. So, the Commonwealth has a population of 2.5 billion on its own with the rest of the 5.5 billion being outside the Commonwealth in countries like China (this being the biggest one, followed by Brazil). Looking at the demographic of Commonwealth citizens outside of Britain, this makes it clear why UK has to have complete control of its borders.

Only recently, the UK Government announced changes to visa fees for Non-UK service members and veterans. While this is a step in the right direction, the new policy still falls short in several areas. Starting this spring, the £2,389 fee for indefinite leave to remain will be waived for Commonwealth personnel who have served a minimum of 6 years or were medically discharged due to service-related injuries or illness. This is down from the initial proposal of a 12-year requirement, which drew widespread criticism. Nearly 7% of UK Armed Forces personnel come from outside Britain, with many hailing from Commonwealth nations like Fiji, Nepal, Africa and Caribbean countries. These men and women leave their homes to serve the UK, making immense sacrifices. Waiving visa fees after several years of service is an acknowledgment of their contributions. However, the new policy excludes family members, who also make significant sacrifices by accompanying soldiers on postings and enduring separations. Campaigners rightly argue that fee waivers should extend to spouses and children. For many Commonwealth veterans, paying thousands in fees to keep their families in the UK after service, remains an unjust financial burden. As one veteran wife put it, "My husband has served this country for over 10 years and I feel it's unfair that we have to pay these huge costs for ourselves and our children to remain." While I'm glad the government has listened to concerns over the proposed 12-year requirement, more needs to be done. The Royal British Legion and other advocates deserve credit for their persistent campaigning on this issue. Their efforts continue, calling on the Government to recognise the integral role families play and include them in fee waivers. Families experience the same strains of service life – it's only right they receive the same consideration when it comes to remaining in the UK after having already paid the 'Right of Passage' to give their service.

Recently, newspapers reported that 70,000 veterans living in Britain could be called up in case of a war. Curious about how many of these veterans are from the Commonwealth and still in the UK, I posted on LinkedIn. I discovered that 17,000 Commonwealth and Gurkha soldiers have left the British Armed Forces in the last five years. Most of them completed their full term of service and have earned the right to remain in the UK, just like anyone else. The comments on my LinkedIn post about Commonwealth soldiers paying visa fees to remain in the UK after service were eye-opening. Many were from UK-born individuals, with some from Commonwealth nations. Reading through, it's clear that no Commonwealth citizen would willingly sacrifice their life for Britain after having to pay exorbitant fees just to gain the right to remain in the country they served. It feels like Britain has lost the affection and broken the trust of Commonwealth soldiers who had to pay to live in the very nation for which they risked their lives. Prior to April 2022, all Commonwealth personnel and Gurkhas leaving service were required to pay a staggering £2,389 per person to apply for indefinite leave to remain (ILR) in the UK, regardless of their length of service. This application fee has since been waived for Commonwealth service members who completed at least 6 years or were medically discharged due to service-related injuries or illnesses. If you have served in the UK for six years, you can apply for naturalisation immediately without needing to apply for indefinite leave to remain. The first five years of your service count towards your residency requirement. However, this process costs £1,850, which is not waived. It's important to note that citizens from certain Commonwealth countries, such as India, Malawi, and Nepal, are not eligible for dual nationality. This means they must renounce their original citizenship if they wish to become British citizens. The recent policy allowing Commonwealth veterans to be exempt from visa fees is a strategic move. While it appears beneficial, it does not change the naturalisation costs or the restrictions on dual nationality for some countries. While this change is a positive step, the majority of Commonwealth veterans are still be charged for their right to citizenship. Campaigners like the Royal British Legion argue the fee waiver should extend to the immediate families of Commonwealth soldiers as well, who make tremendous sacrifices during their loved ones' service. The campaign continues as I write this book. Speaking with groups who left before the new rules, they all feel betrayed by the 'Non-UK' label now applied to Commonwealth veterans.

As one LinkedIn follower poignantly stated: "Britain has backstabbed them once again, just as it did the Windrush Generation, and as we saw after victory was declared in WW1 after they gave their service." If I were to include the individual experiences of each Commonwealth veteran and their families impacted by these policies, we would need an entire series of books to do them justice

Chapter Eight

Getting British Naturalised as a Commonwealth Veteran Experience

A few months ago, someone on my LinkedIn post commented: "Well, you are free to go home after serving. You don't have to stay in England." As a Commonwealth soldier who has served in the British Armed Forces, I've encountered some misconceptions about our motivations and experiences. This oversimplified view fails to grasp the unique challenges we face, including the complex history and personal sacrifices involved. Britain has long relied on Commonwealth nations during times of war. In World War 1, over 1 million volunteers came from India alone. This number swelled to over 2 million in World War 2 – the largest volunteer army in history. We also saw Caribbean volunteers in 1944 – 211 Fijians, and our Gurkha brothers, who have fought alongside British forces for an astounding 212 years. These brave men and women didn't just come to support a foreign land, they came to defend what they saw as their motherland and uphold the Crown's values. Many made the ultimate sacrifice, giving their lives on distant battlefields? So why would a Commonwealth citizen serve, risking injury or death, only to return to what one may call their home?

Only recently, the path to British citizenship for Commonwealth soldiers was far from straightforward. In 2006, I attempted to apply for indefinite leave to remain, only to have my application returned. The exemption stamp on my passport under the Immigration Act 1971 stated that I needed indefinite leave before applying for naturalisation – a classic Catch-22 situation. The process was not just stressful and uncertain, but also took a toll on my emotional and psychological wellbeing. I eventually gained citizenship in 2008 after paying the appropriate fees for myself. However, many of my fellow Commonwealth soldiers weren't so fortunate, forced to abandon their dreams of citizenship or face difficult life choices. Even today, Commonwealth soldiers must meet some of the standard citizenship requirements:

- Living in the UK for 5 years
- Having a clean criminal record
- Demonstrating good character
- Proving English language proficiency*
- Passing the "Life in the UK" test, which assesses an individual's knowledge of British traditions, customs, and history *

The right to citizenship for those who have worn the British uniform and served alongside British nationals should be straightforward. As I write, the last two on this list are no longer required. Today, when I look at the naturalisation process, Britain's process remains one of the most liberal in the world; more liberal than France's, for example. So why is everyone who served more than six years not given naturalisation when we've put our lives on the line, faced the possibility of injury or death, and demonstrated our commitment to Britain by joining the reserve? The path to British belonging still remains complex and uncertain for many. As this debate continues, it's crucial to remember the long history of Commonwealth contributions to British security and the personal sacrifices made by those who choose to serve. We aren't simply looking for an easy path to citizenship – we're seeking recognition for our service and the chance to fully belong in the country we've sworn to protect and serve.

This is a hot topic, one which many of my fellow British colleagues feel strongly about as they see us as equal. In this chapter, we will not only look at the Commonwealth experience in the UK, but also at Gurkhas' experience in Britain.

Even today, naturalisation is not automatic for anyone who came to the UK, wore a British uniform and served alongside other British nationals.

Surely you would think this must be the easiest channel for someone to be considered for the 'Right to Belong'? I use the term 'Right to Belong' here because, unlike any other skilled migrant pathway that is also available to another Commonwealth citizen, this one is about putting your life at risk, the possibility of losing a limb, and death in the line of duty – all of which are a real possibility. In 2006, I went to apply for my indefinite leave to remain, a status that allows a person to live and work in the UK without any restrictions. Still, the form was returned and fees were lost as the exemption stamp on my passport under 'the Immigration Act 1971 Section 4' stated you need to leave the military before you can gain naturalisation – something that my first-born daughter already had (she was also a British citizen based on the fact that she was born whilst I was serving the Crown). Although I was able to apply for my naturalisation in December 2007 and subsequently became a British citizen a few months later, after paying £735 for myself and my wife, this whole process was very stressful as you don't know if you are going to get approved or rejected. Many Commonwealth families during that time were not so lucky and eventually abandoned the process. They had no further option but to go underground or go back home. Even though we served in the British Army, Commonwealth soldiers still needed to meet the standard requirements for British citizenship. This included living in the UK for a certain amount of time (usually 5 years), having no criminal record, demonstrating a good character, proving knowledge of English, and passing a "Life in the UK" test. As a Commonwealth applicant, we have additional hurdles in order to remain in the UK: we must first get indefinite leave before applying for British citizenship as long as our country of birth allows us to have dual nationalities. This was the challenge back then, but when did this all start? To answer this, we may have to go back a few years to 1944, as this was the first time Commonwealth Caribbeans travelled to Britain to join the Armed Forces.

Prior to 1948, Britain functioned like a single, sprawling nation with open borders. Subjects across its vast territories enjoyed a remarkable degree of freedom of movement. People could travel and settle throughout the Empire, including in the United Kingdom, with no bureaucratic hurdles or nationality checks. This reflected the deep political and cultural ties that bound the Empire together. However, the post-War world brought about significant changes, and the free movement of people within the Empire became a relic of the past. This all changed with the introduction of the British Nationality Act 1948 which came into effect on 1 January 1949. This defined the status of "British subject" to include any citizen of the United Kingdom and Colonies (CUKC) or citizen of an independent Commonwealth country.

According to research by 1944, around 4,000 Caribbean volunteers had been recruited to form the dedicated Caribbean Regiment of the British Army. This Caribbean Regiment trained in the U.S. before deploying overseas to Italy, Egypt and Palestine in July 1944. In addition to the Caribbean Regiment, nearly 10,000 other British West Indians had made their own way to the UK by 1944 to enlist individually into the British Army. Many of them married locally and invited their friends to join them in the UK. Hence, the new British Nationality Act of 1948.

During that time the African continent was also very busy, and I remember my grandfather talking about his time in Egypt serving with the British Army under the Mauritius Regiment. Most returned back to their home countries living on their reduced army pension – a similar situation to the Gurkhas' reduced pension in the Nepal before them. Although his pension was not large, my grandfather Murday T. Reddy was able to live on this wage and will always be buying our Christmas gift with it.

So, automatically, those who arrived before 1948 were British subjects. However, there is quite a significant difference being a British subject to being a British citizen and British Commonwealth / Overseas citizen. This is when the confusion started, just like in the case of Anthony Willams who came to the UK at the age of 7 to join his parents in 1971, and later served in the Royal Artillery for 13 years. In 2013, he was wrongly labelled as an illegal immigrant and was sacked from his successful second career as a fitness instructor. Anthony spent five years destitute – because Job Centre records had categorised him as an unlawful resident, he was neither able to work nor claim unemployment benefit.

When he got a tooth infection Anthony was also unable to visit a doctor or dentist. The infection spread until all his top teeth fell out, then most of his lower teeth too. This is one of several experiences of Commonwealth veterans facing bad administration in Britain.

Sadly, as I write this book, Anthony passed away in Jamaica at the age of 60 due to liver cancer. He relocated there in 2023 looking for a fresh start despite 51 years in the UK. You can read about his longstanding battle by searching for him and the people who have courageously supported him. Williams' case exemplifies how the "hostile environment" policy wrongly targeted and devastated the lives of Commonwealth-born veterans who had served the British military loyally. As of September 2021, only 864 people had received compensation out of an initial Home Office estimate of around 15,000 potentially eligible claimants. Anthony sat down and cried when he opened the envelope containing the first compensation offer of £18,500. He had to appeal twice before accepting a higher undisclosed settlement. Even so, he never felt that his compensation was enough due to the lengthy battle he had to endure in a process that he said was intended to make him go away quietly. (https://youtu.be/rhLbbdwU8gw?si=8nWcrMxY_EK9YkEg)

In 1981, the British Nationality Act came in, followed by the 2002 Nationality and Asylum Act, which I have covered in Part One of this book.

Like Anthony, many Commonwealth personnel from the 1998 cohort came to the UK as the 5-year residency rule for Commonwealth citizens was suspended, allowing them to join without having lived in the UK. Prior to 1998, all Commonwealth applicants had to meet a 5-year UK residency requirement before being accepted. So now we have a new cohort joining the British Army Forces as Commonwealth citizens and fighting alongside British personnel. I was part of this cohort to join the British Army in 2001 – after my shift at Buckingham Palace, I walked into the Army Careers Information Office on The Strand, near Trafalgar Square, to become a Royal Fusilier.

Many others joined like me and, unlike me, didn't get cold itchy feet and served their full-term. Tom is one such guy who recently joined our Foundation Programme. I recently met Tom at our Op Belonging United Churches' Service in Tidworth Garrisons, an event that was hugely supported by the Garrison Commander and the local churches in the area. Tom has proudly served the British Army for 23 years, also as a Royal Fusilier, to become the first warrant officer in our cohort but is still not naturalised. Working with him made me really appreciate the sacrifices made by him and his family. However, during our Foundation Programme which is targeted for Commonwealth and Gurkhas, I found out Tom still has to get naturalised and this process will cost him over £1500. In April 2023, the Government announced that all fees for indefinite leave to remain will no longer apply for Commonwealth and Gurkhas personnel. But they still have not removed the naturalisation fees. Tom and I joined around the same time: he came to Litchfield in November 2001, while I had arrived in October 2001. Even if the fees were £1, I still think he should have been given his automatic right to naturalisation as part of his leaving ceremony. Dan Brooks, a reservist in the British Army, has led a campaign for automatic right to citizenship for Commonwealth soldiers for the past three years on 38degrees.org.uk, achieving over 17,000 signatures. If this campaign succeeds, it will remove the humiliation of a serving soldier having to retake the Oath of Allegiance to the Crown which he took 23 years previously!

Similarly, Moses, a fellow Commonwealth soldier who completed his full service, was recently naturalised at Southampton Civic Centre. Having served alongside him in the Royal Logistics, I am immensely proud of his achievement. However, it puzzles me why a Commonwealth soldier, who has already sworn an Oath of Allegiance to the King and Country at the start of his military career, must take the oath again during the naturalisation process. This seems to be an unnecessary repetition and highlights once again a process without principle that could be easily rectified.

Chapter Nine

Health and Wellbeing

As I sit here, reflecting on a recent dinner with our dear friends Ruth and Ian, I'm struck by the complexities of life after military service. Despite their warm smiles and easy conversation, there's a depth to their story that speaks volumes about the challenges veterans and their families face. A House of Lords' report in 2023 revealed a sobering statistic: 33% of surveyed veterans in the UK struggle to adjust to civilian life. It's a number that hits close to home, especially when you know the faces behind the figures. Ruth and Ian, two brave souls, are pillars of our community. Ian, with his crisp Southern British accent, serves as a trustee on several boards. Ruth, a retired community nurse, still volunteers her time, and her gentle Welsh lilt comforts those she helps. They're the kind of couple you'd never suspect harboured a deep, personal connection to the struggles of military transition. Ruth and Ian invited my wife and I to their home for dinner in true British fashion. It's a cultural touchstone in Britain – inviting someone into your home is a gesture of genuine friendship, far more personal than inviting someone to a high-end restaurant. Little did we know that this invitation would open a window into a world we hadn't fully understood before.

During our first real conversation, Ian spoke quietly about his two sons, both veterans of the British Army. The pain in his voice was palpable. Despite being back home, surrounded by family, friends, and their lifelong church community, both sons have struggled to reintegrate and share their experiences. This struggle isn't unique to Ian and Ruth's family. As a veteran, having served in Op Telic and Op Herrick, I've seen this same story repeatedly among my cohorts. The difficulty in re-adjusting and sharing experiences with those who haven't served is a sad and terrible reality for many of us. As we continue to enjoy our friendship with Ruth and Ian, I'm reminded of the importance of understanding and supporting our veterans. Their struggles may not always be visible, but they're genuine. It's up to all of us – friends, family and community members – to create spaces where veterans feel comfortable sharing their experiences and finding the support they need. The journey from military to civilian life is rarely smooth. Still, with compassion, understanding, and most importantly, open dialogue, we can help make that transition more accessible for those who've served our country.

The mental health challenges faced by veterans, especially those from Commonwealth countries, are often overlooked and misunderstood. About 10% of veterans require treatment for Post-Traumatic Stress Disorder (PTSD), struggling with traumatic memories from their service and the loss of comrades in battle. This is a significant issue for many Commonwealth veterans and, unfortunately, as Ian pointed out, the military hasn't always effectively supported those in need. I've seen this firsthand through interactions with numerous veterans in similar situations. One such veteran is James, who lives in Scotland, where accommodation is provided by a local charity. Before his discharge in 2015, James had a happy life with his wife and two young boys. He served in a Scottish regiment but began experiencing mental health issues after leaving the military. When he sought help from his local NHS branch, they weren't well-equipped to support him. Eventually diagnosed with PTSD, James now experiences unpredictable mood swings. During our conversations in Edinburgh, and later over Zoom, it was clear that James was struggling. He was often agitated, and while I'm not a mental health expert, I realised that before we could focus on his career progression, we needed to address his underlying mental health issues. James's story reminds me of hundreds of Commonwealth veterans suffering in silence. Many hesitate to come forward because British society often fails to understand their unique experiences and challenges. It's crucial that we, as a society, strive to understand and support these individuals. Recently, I read a report published by RAND Europe titled "Understanding the Lived Experience of Military to Civilian Transition and Post-Service Life Among Non-UK Veterans." While this 90-page document provides an academic perspective on these challenges, it's concerning that it consistently uses the label "Non-UK" to describe Commonwealth and Gurkha veterans who served and now live in the UK. This terminology feels dismissive of their service and contributions and I'll discuss this issue further in Part Three of this book.

On 20 February 2024, a young man from Ghana contacted me on LinkedIn. His profile picture showed him wearing a beret and displaying his medals. From his career history, it seemed he had run a business at some point, but his current job was unclear. He had seen my post about the campaign urging the UK Government to stop referring to Commonwealth veterans and service personnel living in the UK as "Non-UK." In his message, he shared that he had been struggling with PTSD and felt unsupported. His wife and daughter are in Ghana, and although his daughter is British, he can't afford another visa for his wife to join him. As a civilian, the rules for bringing his partner to the UK have recently changed, making it even harder for him. As a father myself, I can't imagine how difficult it must be for him to suffer alone without support. We eventually had a virtual meeting since he lived far away, and I wanted to hear his story. He was lively during our first Zoom call and mentioned his dream of visiting Mauritius. I encouraged him, saying it was possible and offered to help him find good places to stay. As our light-hearted conversation became more serious, I asked about his current situation. He had his papers, which was a relief because the UK can be hostile without the right to remain. He told me he was a chef and had run his own restaurant in the Midlands until his mental health deteriorated. At this point, he started to cry and became agitated, his struggle becoming more evident.

I had never experienced this before, being on a Zoom call with someone in such distress. When he first messaged me a few weeks before, I was at an event at Silverstone organised by Mission Motorsport. It was one of the most significant military events, and I was listening to the then Veteran Minister's speech about how great Britain is. Yet, here was a man on LinkedIn asking for help and completely lost in the system. To my left of the podium, I saw stands from the Royal British Legion, Help for Heroes, Defence Welfare Medical Services, and other vital organizations showcasing their work. I said to myself: If someone needed help, this was the place to get it. I soon realised how wrong I was. I first approached a lady at the Defence Medical Welfare Service (DMWS) stand, who was very accommodating and took my email. She got in touch a week later. On that day, she introduced me to someone from Help for Heroes, who, after listening to me, passed me on to a colleague who showed me their contact webpage. By then, I was already frustrated: why should someone in need have to fill out a form online when help was right there? It turns out that 90% of charities and organisations supporting veterans hide behind a system. It's all about the system and procedures once again, without having a person-centric approach. I walked away from the stand without a firm contact, except for the lady from the DMWS, who is still engaging with me for other support.

Meanwhile, this young Ghanaian brother is still searching for a way out.

Recently, I spoke at the Army Welfare Service in the South West and saw firsthand how effective the system can be. The Army goes above and beyond to support its people, but this should be a standard service to ensure families are well looked after. The real problem is life after service. People get so accustomed to constant support and find it difficult to adjust to civilian life, and for Commonwealth veterans it's ten times harder. This is where regimental associations can play a vital role after their service. For example, my first regiment, the Royal Regiment of

Fusiliers, has partnered with Leafyard, an online tool to support veterans in managing mental health. They were the first to provide these subscriptions to all their veterans across the UK. On one of my visits to the headquarters, Major Paul Martin, who is a representative for the South West, gave me some cards to distribute. Paul has a great heart for the Commonwealth since 2001, when he wrote his dissertation on Fijians in the British Army. People like him give me hope that it is people, and not process, that will reinvent the Commonwealth experience in Britain through taking a value and principles approach. This underscores the importance of personal support in empowering individuals to make a difference.

Chapter Ten

Relocation

As a young man growing up on the small island of Mauritius in the middle of the Indian Ocean, I dreamt of being part of something bigger than myself. The world beyond my island's shores called to me, promising adventure and opportunity. I yearned to spread my wings and fly, to explore the vast possibilities that lay beyond the horizon. One day, I made a life-changing decision. I would reinvent myself as a soldier and join the British Army. This bold move would not only allow me to serve a greater purpose but also provide a path to settle in the United Kingdom. With a mix of excitement and trepidation, I embarked on this new journey, leaving behind the familiar comforts of home for the unknown challenges ahead. As I adapted to life in the UK, I quickly learned that relocation was not an easy feat. Whether you're an immigrant like me, an expat, or a digital nomad working remotely from exotic locations, the challenges of settling in a new country are universal. It's not just about finding a place to live or securing a job; it's about forging a sense of belonging in an unfamiliar land. Throughout my journey, I discovered that regardless of our skills or backgrounds, we all have a shared common desire when we relocate: to feel a part of something and to build deeper connections with the people around us. This realisation became the cornerstone of my book, "*Leavers to Leaders,*" where I share my experiences and insights on how anyone can successfully navigate the transition to a new life in a foreign land. My story is just one among many, but it illustrates the universal human desire to grow, to challenge ourselves, and to find our place in the world. Whether we're leaving a small island or a bustling metropolis, the quest for belonging and connection remains at the heart of our journey.

Jilly's world shattered in an instant when her husband, Colonel Nick Carrell, was diagnosed with an aggressive form of brain cancer. As a military family living in service accommodation, they had built a life together – a home filled with love, laughter, and the pitter-patter of their two daughters, four dogs, and two cats. Nick was still actively serving in the military when the unthinkable happened – he passed away, leaving Jilly and their children to navigate a sea of grief. But their pain was compounded by a harsh reality of military life. Despite their loss, Jilly and her family were given just 93 days to vacate their home. The place where they had made countless memories, where their children had grown up, where they had weathered life's storms together, was no longer theirs to call home. As Jilly shared her story at an NHS Berkshire event, her words painted a vivid picture of the challenges faced by bereaved military families. The audience listened in stunned silence as she described the whirlwind of emotions – the overwhelming grief of losing her husband, the stress of finding a new home, the heartache of uprooting her children from their schools and friends, all while trying to process their immense loss. Her story struck a deep chord with me. As someone who experienced bereavement at the young age of 22, I could relate to the trauma of losing a loved one. Even though it's been nearly 25 years since my own loss, listening to Jilly's experience brought tears to my eyes, reminding me that some wounds never fully heal. Jilly's mission now is to raise awareness about the lives of military families with children after the bereavement of a service member. Her lived experience, which she bravely shares on social media, sheds light on a little-known aspect of military life. It's a shocking reminder of the sacrifices made not just by service members, but by their families as well. Through her advocacy, Jilly hopes to bring about change, to ensure that bereaved military families are given the time and support they need to grieve and rebuild their lives. Her story is a powerful testament to the resilience of the human spirit and a call to action for better support systems for those who have given so much in service to their country.

This situation has been even more complex for Commonwealth families who lost their partner during the Iraq or Afghanistan conflict. One of them is the family of Private Pita Tukutukuwaqa who died on 8 November 2004 when his Warrior armoured vehicle was hit by a roadside improvised explosive device making it 20 years ago this year. He was married and his wife returned to the capital of Fiji, Suva, after his death. Like him, many Commonwealth soldiers lost their lives in battle alongside our British Comrades. According to an article by The Independent, 179 British soldiers died in the Iraq War Op Telic: each of those members' families have had to experience tragic relocations after their partners were killed in action.

Atta Junior and Atta Senior, twin Commonwealth brothers from Ghana, shared with me their own struggles of having to find accommodation and relocating after their service. One of them served in the Royal Logistics and the other in the Green Jackets. Unlike our British counterparts, we do not have an uncle in Scotland or a childhood friend in Wales who we can reconnect with to ease the relocation. Commonwealth soldiers have to first decide where they would like to live, and this is a huge problem since we know little about our surroundings. When you are in the military, your life is mostly behind the wire with little connection with the town or village you are in – most Barracks are in the middle of nowhere with awful reception, something I came to realise a long time ago. Take Tidworth Garrison for example: to the east we have Basingstoke (which is 40 miles away), west is Bristol (also 40 miles away) and Salisbury (10 miles away), followed by Southampton. As a family, if you are based in Salisbury Plain, then you have quite a few options, not forgetting Swindon which is already heavily populated with veterans. Like most service leavers, you have the added responsibility to ensure your family, your spouse and children can easily integrate in a community – hence why these cities offer a welcoming space as, more than likely, you will not be the only coloured person walking around town. Other villages can be hard to integrate in, even across Scotland, where according to Eddie – an executive lecturer for higher education born and bred in Scotland – it can take up to three generations to fully belong around the Tayside.

First Lady Michelle Obama said it best in her interview with Variety magazine, when she emphasised the significance of diverse representation in the media. She stated, "For so many people, television and movies may be the only way they understand people who aren't like them." This highlights her belief in the power of seeing diverse faces and stories in popular culture – a vital part of our Operation Belonging.

On a warm summer afternoon, the aroma of spices and sizzling meat filled the air as Tony, a tall Jamaican veteran, expertly manned the grill. His passion for jerk chicken was unmatched, and I couldn't help but think he could have been a Masterchef contender if only I had been able to help him transition back to civilian life in 2009. Unfortunately, I was then myself trying to navigate the struggles of transition in Britain. After leaving the British Army, Tony and his family settled in Whiteleigh, near Fareham, a small town on the South West Coast of England. Despite its proximity to Southampton, Tony struggled to integrate into the community with his Jamaican family. His children faced bullying at school, and neighbours complained about the frequent barbecues, the aromatic smells, the lively music, and the steady stream of visitors. Tony remained popular among his former army comrades from Portsmouth, finding solace in those connections. His love for driving led him to become an HGV driver, but the long days on the road took their toll. Coming home each night became less and less pleasant as the neighbourhood's hostility grew. Tony's wife, isolated and unable to make friends, felt the strain acutely; they were the only Black family in the village. Fortunately, as renters, they weren't tied to the area. After a few difficult years, Tony and his family made the difficult decision to leave the UK for Canada. There, Tony found work as a long-haul truck driver and finally began to settle into a more welcoming community. Years later, whenever I fire up the grill, I'm reminded of Tony's masterful jerk chicken and the life lessons he taught me. His story echoes the experiences of many Caribbean immigrants who arrived in 1948, struggling to find their place after hanging up their military uniforms. Tony's journey highlights the challenges faced by Commonwealth veterans when relocating to new communities. Too often, these loyal servicemen and women who came to Britain with a purpose remain unseen and unheard. When was the last time we saw a Commonwealth soldier, aviator, or sailor proudly wearing their uniform in public? Perhaps it's time to raise awareness about this small but significant community of citizens who served Britain with unwavering loyalty. Their stories, like Tony's, deserve to be told and their contributions recognised, ensuring that future generations of Commonwealth veterans find the welcome and support they've earned through their service.

As I sat down to write this chapter, my phone rang. It was Rama, an old friend from my days in the Royal Logistics. We hadn't seen each other since his wedding in 2007, but his voice brought back a flood of memories. Rama was an Indo-Fijian, a rarity in the military circles we moved in. I remembered him as a skilled mechanic, always ready to lend a hand. He had fixed my car more times than I could count. Our shared South Indian heritage from indentureship of our ancestors gave us a unique bond, a connection that went beyond our military service. As we caught up, Rama told me about his life since leaving the Army. He had married an English girl and together they had bought a house on the outskirts of the New Forest. Like many ex-servicemen, he had become an HGV driver. I could hear the contentment in his voice as he described their life in the picturesque countryside. Our conversation made me reflect on the different paths taken by Commonwealth veterans in the UK. Rama's story was one of successful integration – embracing English life while maintaining his cultural identity. It was a stark contrast to some of the struggles I had witnessed among other veterans. This year marks a significant milestone for me – I will have lived half my life in Mauritius and half in England. This dual perspective has given me a unique lens through which to view the world. I see things from a Mauritian angle, a British angle, and a third angle that blends both. I've come to call this perspective "third culture leadership." My own family embodies this hybrid identity. We feel British but live an English life with a Mauritian flavour. My daughters, like many children of Commonwealth immigrants born in the UK, feel more British than English. It's a nuanced distinction, but an important one. In our Young Leavers to Leaders programme, which guides teenagers into adulthood, we often discuss the concept of belonging. The fresh perspectives of these young people never fail to enlighten me.

As I hung up the phone with Rama, I pondered a crucial question: who is responsible for preparing communities to welcome those who have served? While I don't believe it's solely the Government's job, I do think each of us who has served has a duty to share our Commonwealth experiences. After all, who better to tell these stories than those who have lived them? Our experiences, our struggles, and our successes are part of the rich tapestry of modern Britain. By sharing them, we not only honour our own journeys but also pave the way for future generations of Commonwealth citizens who choose to serve. It's a responsibility we must embrace for the sake of those who will follow in our footsteps.

Chapter Eleven

Local Authorities and Armed Forces Covenant

It all started back in 2000 when the UK Ministry of Defence put out this booklet called "Soldiering – The Military Covenant." It talked about this idea of a "Military Covenant" or "Armed Forces Covenant" – basically, the mutual obligations between the nation and its Armed Forces personnel. But at that point, it was just a concept on paper, nothing legally binding. The Covenant didn't really gain much traction until General Sir Richard Dannatt took over as Chief of the General Staff in 2006. He was a big champion of the idea, really pushing it into the political spotlight. Even so, it still didn't have any legal force behind it – it was just a set of principles.

I remember around that time, there was a group of Gurkhas protesting in the UK about their pensions. I was just a young, newly recruited soldier myself back then, maybe a bit naive to fully understand the complexities of their situation and transition. But I do recall hoping that Commonwealth veterans, and even myself down the line, wouldn't face similar treatment. From what I understand now, that particular group of Gurkha protesters was affected by the changes made by the Labour Government between 1997 and 2003. It was a very specific issue related to a small group of Gurkha pensioners who had been part of the 1947 pension scheme. That older scheme apparently had some different advantages compared to the newer Armed Forces Pension Scheme that Gurkhas were transferred to during that 1997–2003 period. So, while the overarching Covenant concept had been introduced, there were still these more granular pension issues being fought over by certain veteran groups like those Gurkha protesters. It really highlighted the complexities involved in upholding that mutual obligation between the nation and its Armed Forces across different eras and pension schemes.

It wasn't until 2011 that the Armed Forces Covenant was officially established. This is when organisations started signing pledges to honour the principles of the Covenant, essentially making a commitment to treat members of the Armed Forces community fairly. While the pledges were a step in the right direction, the Covenant still lacked legal teeth. That finally changed in November 2022 when the Covenant Legal Duty came into force. This places a legal obligation on certain public bodies, like those dealing with healthcare, education, and housing, to actively consider the Covenant principles when carrying out their duties related to the Armed Forces community. While the concept emerged in 2000, it took over 20 years for the Armed Forces Covenant to go from just an idea to an actual legally binding requirement for public bodies. The journey from principle to law was a long one, but an important milestone for the UK's commitment to its Armed Forces personnel and veterans. My first real experience about the practicality of the Covenant for Commonwealth Veterans was late last year when I came across Timi (not his real name), a veteran with 12 years of service, who lived in the South. Although there are a lot of skill-upgrading courses offered by the council, they would not even consider the case of Timi. Why, you may ask? Well, Timi was one of those who had no money to apply for his indefinite leave to remain after discharge. He became an 'alien' (a term which I describe earlier in this book), according to a reply I had from a city council manager who was supposed to be an Armed Forces champion. It seemed to be that even though Timi served, they are not able to support him or even look into his situation because of his immigration status. They simply were not interested to know any further. This situation has since then made me think deeply about how the Armed Forces Covenant is supporting Commonwealth citizens across Britain. As Iveri would say to me (his story from soldier to care manager is later in this book): 'How much more do we have to do as Commonwealth; how much more do we have to give in order to be respected in Britain?' This is the main motive behind this book, and I hope to be able to raise more awareness of this.

Another time that really made me think of the Covenant was when a local charity contacted me about a Ghanaian veteran who was sleeping in his car as he had lost his business. Because he did not have a British Passport, the council (which was in the North East), was unable to support him. What is going on? Why is there a requirement of a British passport to get support from the local authority? Are they not aware of the Covenant? This case was last year and clearly there is a lack of knowledge among local authorities who have signed the Covenant with the majority being White British while the minority are ignored. As a seasoned Commonwealth veteran living in England, I am yet to see the reward or benefits in the Covenant. No one has come forward to say: 'I got this help from the Covenant: the job I got was due to the Covenant.' Unless there is provision for Commonwealth, Gurkhas and those from Overseas British Territories, I doubt we will see a truly inclusive community where Commonwealth citizens can belong.

Ronn had served in the British Army for 10 years, proudly representing his home country of Jamaica. When he left the service, he was excited to start a new chapter in England, the country he had grown to love during his time in uniform. However, the transition to civilian life proved more challenging than he had anticipated. At first, Ronn struggled to find steady employment. His military skills didn't seem to translate well to the civilian job market, and he found himself taking odd jobs to make ends meet. As the months went by, his savings dwindled and he began to fall behind on rent payments for his small flat. Desperate for help, Ronn reached out to his local council hoping they might have resources for veterans like himself. To his dismay, he discovered that his local authority, like many others in England, had no specific provisions for veterans in their housing strategy. The staff seemed unsure how to assist him, despite his service to the country. Ronn's story is not unique. According to a recent analysis by the No Homeless Veterans campaign, 252 out of 343 local authorities in England do not include veterans in their housing strategies. Even more concerning, 176 fail to consider the needs of veterans in their homelessness strategies, despite clear guidance in the Homelessness Code of Guidance.

As Ronn's situation worsened, he found himself sleeping on friends' couches, then eventually in his car. He felt invisible: a Commonwealth veteran who had served the UK faithfully, now struggling to find his place in civilian society. Each setback seemed to chip away at his confidence and ability to move forward. Ronn's experience highlights a critical gap in support for veterans, especially those from Commonwealth countries. For many like Ronn, it only takes one or two unfortunate decisions or circumstances to spiral into homelessness. Without targeted support and understanding from local authorities, these veterans often struggle to develop the life skills needed to regain their footing and move forward. As Ronn sat in his car one cold night, he couldn't help but wonder: if local authorities had been better prepared to support veterans like himself, could his story have turned out differently? The answer, hidden in the statistics and strategies of councils across England, remains a sobering reminder of the work still needed to ensure no veteran is left behind.

Chapter Twelve

Britain and the National Health Service

'We need you to pull over and stay on the phone with us while we drive to you.'

The blue lights flashed in my rear-view mirror and embarrassment washed over me. In nearly 15 years of living in the UK, this was my first call to 999. I had pulled over on the famous A27 from Brighton, about 60 miles from home, when I realised something was wrong. The emergency responders arrived in less than ten minutes. As they helped me out of the car and onto a stretcher, I couldn't help but think how ridiculous this whole situation felt. The ex-squaddie in me insisted I was okay and could just drive home. It's an ingrained mentality – you can survive if you're not dying. After checking my vitals, the responders gave me two options: leave my car by the roadside (absolutely not) or drive to my local hospital.

I chose the latter, but I was still convinced I was overreacting. Little did I know, I was about to embark on a two-week stay at Southampton General Hospital, recovering from a rare condition called bilateral Bell's palsy – affecting only one in five million people. Lucky me.

During my stay, I gained a profound respect for the NHS and its staff, particularly the foreign and Commonwealth workers who keep it running. Unable to speak, move my face, or even close my eyes at night, I found myself in Ward D, as the neuro ward was entirely full. Being a university hospital, Southampton General became a parade ground of young medical students eager to examine me. They had me perform experimental walks and balance exercises, such as walking in a straight line and standing on one leg, touching this and that with my left and right arms to test my coordination and muscle strength. Among the nurses was the wife of a Commonwealth soldier from Ghana who knew my wife. She took excellent care of me and even texted my wife to assure her I was in good hands. With pen and paper as my only means of communication, I asked her about her husband's service and how many other Commonwealth military families she knew working for the NHS.

"There are loads of us," she replied. "Most are bank staff as it's the most flexible rota when you have a husband in the military." As I lay there, unable to speak but observing everything around me, I realised the incredible diversity and dedication of the NHS staff. It was a humbling experience that gave me a new appreciation for the healthcare system and the people who make it work, especially those who, like me, had come from far away to serve in a new home.

In 2022, a survey by the NHS showed that 49.9 % of the hospital and community health services (HCHS) doctors were from an ethnic background, 15.0% of people in managerial level positions, and 11.3% of senior managerial level positions. Over the next few days, I recced the whole hospital, and got to know people from the senior consultant 'Mary' to the junior staff at the neuro department on the other side of the building. Southampton General is a massive hospital; it was built in 1900 and has since continued to get bigger and bigger. At the time, in 2017, it had over 12,000 people looking after 4 million patients across the South and the neuro unit is very well known and people would travel as far as Jersey for major operations. It was the first time I have experienced such a diverse organisation made up of so many people who have travelled to the UK to serve this nation, just like Commonwealth and Gurkhas soldiers. This was way before Boris Johnson and his administration made a joke out of them during Covid.

In 2001, two young men from different Commonwealth countries joined the British Army, their paths seemingly parallel. But a decade later, their experiences with the UK's National Health Service (NHS) would diverge dramatically, revealing a troubling disparity in how Britain treats its veterans. Taitusi Ratucaucau, a Fijian-born soldier, left the military in 2011 after more than a decade of service, including tours in Belize and the Falklands.

He settled in the UK with his family, paying taxes and National Insurance like any other resident. But in 2020, Ratucaucau's world was turned upside down when he collapsed and was diagnosed with a brain tumor requiring immediate surgery. What should have been a time of recovery and support turned into a nightmare. Despite his years of service to the Crown, a hospital staff member classified Ratucaucau as an "overseas patient." This bureaucratic decision left him facing a staggering bill of nearly £30,000, increasing by £1,500 each day he remained in the hospital. The news sent shockwaves through the military community. How could Britain, a country proud of its NHS and its Armed Forces, charge a former soldier for life-saving treatment? This wasn't America, where health insurance is a prerequisite for care. This was Britain, charging a veteran who had risked his life for the country, for every penny of his brain surgery. In a heart-wrenching interview with the BBC, Ratucaucau expressed his shock and disillusionment:

"If I knew it was going to be like this, I would never have come here." The incident exposed a glaring issue in the system.
(https://inews.co.uk/news/british-army-veteran-taitusi-ratucaucau-nhs-bill-life-saving-brain-operation-432175)

Ratucaucau had served for more than the five years as required for indefinite leave to remain, yet found himself caught in an immigration limbo that left him vulnerable to such treatment. It was a wake-up call, revealing a problem that had been simmering beneath the surface for years, known to many but addressed by few. His story serves as a shocking reminder of the complexities and often harsh realities faced by

Commonwealth veterans in the UK. It highlights the urgent need to reinvent how Britain treats those who have served, regardless of their place of birth. The immigration issues that led to this situation are complex and deeply rooted, deserving of careful examination and swift action to prevent such injustices from occurring again. This is why we need to re-examine the Commonwealth experience in Britain and the process that has underpinned it for the best part of eighty years.

Ratucaucau's experience stands as a testament to the sacrifices made by Commonwealth soldiers and the unexpected battles they sometimes face long after leaving the battlefield. It calls into question the very nature of service, citizenship, and the responsibility a nation has to those who have sworn to defend it.

Today, NHS England has made a promise to look after every veteran under the two banners Op Courage and Op Restore and to ensure their families are also looked after. Perhaps a simple conversation as part of the patient administration process would have been to ask patients: 'Are you part of the Armed Forces community?' or 'Have you served?' This would have saved a lot of trouble and stress for Ratucaucau and his family. It is most important for NHS staff to understand that the UK Armed Forces have recruited over 100,000 Commonwealth and Foreign nationals who are living in the UK. It is essential to become more culturally aware that the British military is a diverse recruitment organisation just like the NHS.

Chapter Thirteen

Home from Home: Housing

On a warm summer evening, I found myself reflecting on the importance of having a place to call home. The thought brought to mind the powerful story depicted in the movie "The Swimmers" based on the true experiences of two sisters from Damascus. Their journey was nothing short of harrowing. Fleeing their war-torn home, they swam for hours in the choppy Mediterranean Sea to reach Greece as asylum seekers. Despite the immense challenges they faced, they went on to compete in the Rio Olympic Games. The story of these sisters, Yusra and Sara Mardini, is a testament to the resilience of the human spirit and the profound need for a place to call home. Their journey began in the chaos of Syria, where their lives were constantly under threat from shelling and sniper attacks. They made the heart-wrenching decision to leave everything behind in search of safety and a new beginning. Their escape was fraught with danger. After reaching Turkey, they boarded a small, overcrowded dinghy with 18 other refugees. When the boat's engine failed and it began to take on water, Yusra and Sara, both strong swimmers, jumped into the sea. For hours, they swam alongside the sinking boat, guiding it to safety and saving the lives of everyone on board.

Their story didn't end there. After reaching Greece, they continued their journey through Europe, facing numerous obstacles along the way. Eventually, they found refuge in Germany, where Yusra's swimming talent was recognised. She was invited to join the Refugee Olympic Team and competed in the 2016 Rio Olympics, bringing hope and inspiration to millions of refugees around the world. The Mardini sisters' story highlights the critical importance of having a place to call home. It's not just about having a roof over your head; it's about having a safe, stable environment where you can build a life, pursue your dreams, and find a sense of belonging. Their journey underscores the challenges faced by those who are forced to leave their homes and the incredible strength it takes to start anew in a foreign land.

As I thought about their story, I realised how vital it is for everyone to have a place they can call home. It's a fundamental human need that provides stability, security, and a foundation for building a better future. The Mardini sisters' journey is a powerful reminder of the resilience of the human spirit and the importance of creating a world where everyone has the opportunity to find a place they can truly call home.

As the sun set over a small military town in England, Amani and her husband Jabari sat on their modest balcony, sipping tea and dreaming of home. It had been two years since they left Kenya to serve in the British Armed Forces and, while they were proud of their decision, they couldn't help but feel a sense of displacement. "Do you think we'll ever truly feel at home here?" Amani asked, her eyes distant as she imagined the rolling hills of her homeland. Jabari squeezed her hand: "I don't know, my love. But we're here now, and we must make the best of it." Their conversation drifted to their plans for the future – not of settling in the UK but of buying land back in Kenya, building a house, purchasing a car. It was a common dream among Commonwealth soldiers, to improve the lives of those they left behind. As the years passed, Amani and Jabari's story became intertwined with hundreds of others like them. Some, like Iveri from Fiji, had saved for years just to join the military, scraping together $5,000 for the opportunity to serve. For the first five years, most focused on sending money home, repaying debts, and supporting family members. But as time wore on, something began to shift. Around the ten-year mark, with families of their own and roots beginning to take hold, many Commonwealth soldiers found themselves at a crossroads.

One evening, at a gathering of veterans, an older Ghanaian soldier named Kwesi shared his experience:

"When I first arrived, all I could think about was going back. But now, after fifteen years, two children born here, and a community that's slowly accepted us ... I'm not so sure anymore."

His words resonated with many in the room. They had come seeking three things: acceptance, a voice, and a place to call home. For some, like Amani and Jabari, these elements remained elusive. For others, like Kwesi, they had found an unexpected sense of belonging.

As the night wore on, conversations flowed, touching on the challenges they faced – the struggle for acceptance, the fight to be heard, the constant question of where "home" truly was. Some spoke of returning to their countries of origin, while others had decided to put down permanent roots in the UK. In the end, there was no single story, no universal experience. Each soldier's journey was unique, shaped by their own struggles, triumphs, and the delicate balance between two worlds. But as they shared their stories, one thing became clear – the path to feeling at home was long and winding, but not impossible. As Amani and Jabari walked home that night, hand in hand, they realised their story was still being written. The question of where they truly belonged remained unanswered, but they found comfort in knowing they weren't alone in their journey.

Atta Senior, a Ghanaian veteran, served in the Royal Logistics Corps from 2002 to 2010. His journey was far from straightforward. Both he and his twin brother, Atta Junior, joined the military at the same time but ended up in different regiments, leading to vastly different experiences. While Junior's story would come later, Atta Senior's tale was one of struggle and resilience. Stationed in Germany, Atta Senior lived with his wife and daughters. The challenges began when he tried to navigate life after the military. Unlike his peers in the UK, he had no guidance on where to live, how to buy a house, or how to sort out his immigration status. The lack of support was glaring and his frustration was palpable.

He often voiced his struggles in his native Ghanaian language, sometimes resorting to swear words to express his exasperation. After much effort and a hefty £1,500 fee to renew his immigration status, Atta Senior and his family finally moved to the UK. "I was looking for someone who had been out before me to ask for advice," he said, reflecting on the isolation he felt during that period. The move to the UK was supposed to be a fresh start, but it came with its own set of challenges. The global financial crisis of 2009 had just hit and finding a job was tough. Both Atta and his wife had to work tirelessly to cover their £1,000 rent, food, and bills. They had a six-month-old baby and a two-year-old son, making the situation even more stressful. Despite the hardships, Atta was grateful for his professional driving qualifications, which he had earned while serving. However, the high cost of living left them with no money to save for a house. This financial trap was a common pitfall for many Commonwealth veterans.

As Atta Senior navigated these challenges, he couldn't help but question the so-called "Commonwealth dream" after military service. Was this what they had signed up for? The dream of improving the lives of their loved ones back home often overshadowed the need to plan for life in the UK. Through conversations with hundreds of Commonwealth veterans, a pattern emerged. The first five years were typically spent sending money back home to repay debts and support family members. But after a decade in the UK, perspectives began to shift. Veterans started to see the UK as a potential home, especially if they had families. They began to grow roots and realise that this country could indeed be their home. Atta Senior's story, like that of many others, highlighted the need for better support systems for Commonwealth veterans. The journey from military service to civilian life was fraught with challenges, but with the right guidance and support it was possible to find a place to call home.

My best advice to those who are thinking of owning a house is to buy and wait – don't wait to buy. It is very clear today that investing in bricks and mortar is one of the safest deals on the market while it also provides a roof over your head. Yes, as a newbie in the UK, you will need to create a successful credit file to be given a mortgage.

It was 2006, and the air was thick with possibility. My wife and I, after years of army life, were ready to plant roots. We decided it was time to buy our first home, a decision that would lead us on an unexpected adventure. Our house-hunting journey felt like we had stepped into one of those reality TV shows. Estate agents bombarded us with emails and phone calls, eager to show us properties in neighbourhoods we had never even heard of. For years, we had lived "behind the wire" on military bases and the civilian world of real estate was an entirely new terrain to navigate. We crisscrossed the country, from North London to Southampton, a vast area that seemed to grow with each property we viewed.

The excitement built as we imagined ourselves in each home, picturing where our furniture would go and which room would be the nursery for our future children. Finally, we found it – a charming house in North London that felt like home the moment we stepped through the door. Our hearts raced as we imagined our life there. This was it, we thought. Our dream was within reach. But then came the shocking blow. Every mortgage lender we approached declined our application. We were baffled. What was wrong with us as buyers? We both had steady incomes from the Army, no debts, and savings for a deposit. Surely, we were ideal candidates? The truth, when we discovered it, was almost comical. It turned out that our prudent financial habits – never having debt, not even a mobile phone contract or a credit card – had worked against us. In the eyes of lenders, we didn't exist. We had no credit history, no proof that we could manage debt responsibly. I remember laughing in disbelief when I realised that in the West, you need to have debts to be given credit. It seemed backwards, almost absurd. Here we were, thinking our lack of debt made us financially responsible, only to find out it made us financial ghosts. Quickly, we had to adapt to this new reality. We applied for credit cards, took out phone contracts, anything to build a credit history. It felt strange, deliberately taking on small debts to prove we could handle larger ones.

Even today, years later, I find this system perplexing. The idea that the less financial commitment you have, the less you can borrow, still strikes me as counterintuitive. It's a lesson we learned the hard way – one that transformed our journey from army life to homeownership into an unexpected crash course in civilian financial norms. Our dream home in North London slipped through our fingers that year, but the experience taught us valuable lessons about navigating the civilian world. It was just the beginning of our adventure in transitioning from military to civilian life; full of surprises, challenges, and ultimately, growth.

Atta Senior and his wife worked tirelessly for three years to save for a deposit and finally bought their house in 2012. "Some people told me it was foolish to leave the army," Senior recalled. "I had two friends who rejoined because they couldn't find a job after eight months out of the military and it's the same today. One of my Ghanaian friends, now a late entry officer (LE) on his way to becoming a Major after 26 years of service, is terrified. He has no experience outside the military and is fast approaching his mid-50s." This is the military trap for many Commonwealth soldiers who extend their military careers beyond their initial terms. A few weeks after my conversation with Senior, I met Yam Roka, a former Gurkha who now runs his own estate agency. He focuses on helping Gurkhas buy houses while still in service, renting and managing them while they are away. This is perhaps one of the best pieces of advice for Commonwealth soldiers and veterans, something that no resettlement service will tell you. Like Atta, today we support those in our Leavers to Leaders programme to get a house as early as possible by connecting them with estate agents in areas they might settle in the future. For Commonwealth soldiers, having a place in Britain is rarely about location; as long as you can rent it, it's a good investment.

Chapter Fourteen

Commonwealth in the Community

'Every time we organise an event, we never get any attendance by the Commonwealth; they don't read orders, emails or anything.' These were the exact words at a Royal Navy Commonwealth symposium in Worth Down organised by the Commonwealth team. This is not the first time I have heard someone saying that. Aldershot Garrison and Tidworth Garrison which are the two major garrisons in the South, have the same problem. One welfare officer who is on his last year with the British Army, and himself a Commonwealth individual, said to me: 'When you do an event, you never know who will show up; it has become very hard for Commonwealth to trust the system.' There you go, he hit the nail on the head: 'trust' and 'system' are the two significant words.

For nearly three years, I was involved in a local awards circuit that spanned England, Wales and Scotland. During this time, I encountered only one other Commonwealth individual. Initially, I attributed this to the locations of the events, but as time passed I realised that Commonwealth veterans were unlikely to feel comfortable attending such award ceremonies, even if they were free—and in the UK, they rarely are. These events have become lucrative businesses, as everyone enjoys being in the spotlight, despite claiming otherwise. Since the rise of individualism which I have covered in my third book *'Reinvented'*, such events have gained popularity across the UK.

It took me almost three years to understand that I was in the wrong crowd. Deep down, I probably knew it all along, especially each time I had to stand on stage to present the *'Leavers to Leaders'* Award. Looking out at the audience, filled with impeccably dressed individuals adorned with shiny medals, I realised I was the only Brown veteran in the room.

Initially, this made me uncomfortable, especially considering it was 2022, yet I was the only non-White veteran present. Over time, I got used to it, much like I had in the academic world, which is now changing rapidly. One of the significant challenges for Commonwealth veterans is adapting to English banter, just like the Scottish or Welsh had to. Though not hurtful, and often a good icebreaker once you get used to it, there have been reports of its inappropriateness. My observation is that British people know very little about the Commonwealth and lately, this has proven to be very poor, when a report for the military stated that officers in the British Army were confused between the Fiji Islands and the Caribbeans.

Winston, who came to the UK with his mum and dad aged 14 in 1967, told me that in those days you had to stay out of trouble, so his parents send him to join the youth club – the Boys' Brigade – which had a military connection. 'The big drop off was in 1974 when Britain joined the Commonwealth market; they stopped importing sugar, bananas, citrus and destroyed the GDP of the Commonwealth.' I really enjoyed meeting Winston. When I first met him with his black suit, light purple shirt and dark grey tie, I honestly thought he was about my age. On the left of his chest, he had a pin with the Jamaica flag – I could tell he was a proud Jamaican. Later, during our conversation, he told me he had served for 29 years and 7 months. I was starting to do the maths in my head – it was clear he was older than me. I asked: 'Why seven months?' He replied: 'In those days, when you were not 18, any time you did was not counted toward your pension.' He joined the RAF at the age of 17 and a half. 'So I gave the Crown six months for free.' It was then that I realised that Winston was old enough to be my big brother or even my dad. He told me: 'I used to look like you.' And here I was thinking he looked much better than me! What he then said has kept me thinking, even now: 'You see I don't drink, I don't smoke, I do regular walks, I eat lots of vegetables and fruits.' Looks like I got my secret remedy here –

and coming from someone who was almost twice my age and looked better than me, I certainly took his advice seriously. We spoke for more than an hour that day and the topic of visas came up. Immigration, visas, and naturalisation are significant issues for us Commonwealth individuals and will be explored in my next book.

We know we are immigrants and without our papers we can be destitute, as many have been. Winston shared, "In those days, we had the Black Power movement. We wouldn't travel overseas for military operations on our island passports." This was in the 1970s. "At one point, we had to go to Mazirah Island. So, we stuck together as a community – no one would leave Britain. There was nothing they could do and we were all issued British passports at the 10th Regiment RAF. So, there we were in the 1970s, Commonwealth citizens living in Britain issued with British passports to travel on operations."

I remember an interview with a Commonwealth officer from South Africa who shared a particularly disheartening experience. After returning from an operation, he had to join the Non-UK national line at passport control at Gatwick. "My soldiers were all wondering what was wrong with me," he said. "Even though I am an officer, it was humiliating to see other Commonwealth soldiers, who had been on the same mission and done the exact same things as their British colleagues, being treated differently when it came to immigration." This stark contrast in treatment highlighted how immigration policies could divide the band of brothers. As he recounted his story, it became clear that the bonds forged in service could be strained by the realities of immigration. "When it comes to it," he continued, "you will have practically no one to fall back on if you suddenly need help. If you manage to face your immigration difficulties and come out on top, good luck to you." His words stayed with me, a poignant reminder of the challenges faced by Commonwealth soldiers who serve alongside their British counterparts on operations but are not afforded the same rights and recognition when they return.

Similarly the majority of Commonwealth individuals are from a Christian background, and many would make an effort to attend a local church in the community. Many churches have coined the idea of 'diversity and inclusivity' or DEI (the buzzwords these days) But you only need to pop your head in the room to notice that there is nothing multicultural about them. It is one community, one culture dominating the service. This is, of course, not how the church leaders see it. I once challenged a church leader about his message of diversity and inclusivity as it felt totally wrong. The organisation put Black and Brown people everywhere where you could see them: on posters, on the 'welcome' doors, and even on the boards. However, the culture in the room had not changed one bit. It is always as if the message is: 'If you can do things the way we do it here, then you are part of the team.' The irony is that there are many people on the other side of this segregated community who also want to see more mixing but feel let down by politics in church.

Ross, a former Royal Navy chef, lives with his wife and two young daughters in a cramped one-bedroom flat in a remote area. After serving for five years in the military, the irregular hours and shift work have taken a toll on his body clock. Now, he struggles to adjust to civilian life and find his place in the local community. Originally from Ghana, Ross joined the Royal Navy with hopes of building a better life in the UK. However, since leaving the service, he's found himself caught in a cycle of low-skilled, low-paid work. Currently, he makes ends meet by doing food deliveries in his old Astra, while still trying to repay credit card debts incurred from securing indefinite leave to remain for himself and his wife last year. Determined to provide a better future for his daughters, Ross believes that integration is key. He understands that to break the cycle of limited opportunities often faced by Commonwealth veterans, his children need to develop social skills by interacting with children from White British families. With this in mind, Ross and his family joined a church in Hedge End, hoping to make friends and find a sense of belonging. However, the reality has been disappointing. Although Ross can see other Ghanaians at the church, he struggles to connect with them due to cultural and social differences.

The church community, while welcoming, seems to lack understanding of the unique experiences and challenges faced by Commonwealth veterans like Ross. Frustrated by the lack of integration, Ross reflects on the broader issue: "There are too many churches who do not have an understanding of British soldiers and veterans from the Commonwealth." He observes that this has led to the creation of nationality-specific churches across the UK, unintentionally promoting segregation rather than integration. Ross believes that mixing people of different races on an equal footing is crucial for a better multicultural Britain. He dreams of a community where his daughters can form friendships with children from diverse backgrounds, including White British families. However, in his current situation, this dream seems far from reality. As Ross continues to navigate life in the UK, he hopes for more understanding and support for Commonwealth veterans in local communities. He believes that by bridging these cultural gaps and promoting genuine integration, churches and other community organisations can play a vital role in creating a more inclusive society for all. After listening to him, it's clear that he feels like Britain has let him down and the Commonwealth dream is far from sight. This attitude unfortunately is what we see happening in key organisations across Britain.

Chapter Fifteen

Education and Work Placement

Why is it difficult to gain further education as a Commonwealth individual in Britain? Back in the 90s, Britain had always been one of the top most desired countries for those from the Commonwealth to come and study. I came here to do the same in 2001. In Mauritius, our GCSE and A Levels have been accredited by Cambridge University since the early 70s. It has always been well recognised globally due to this fact. But other Commonwealth countries are big enough to invest in their own accreditation system.

The UK has long been a popular destination for students from around the globe seeking a world-class education. In recent years, the influx of international students has hit record highs. In the 2021/22 academic year, a whopping 679,970 international students were pursuing their studies at universities across the United Kingdom. That's an incredible 37% increase compared to just three years prior! To break it down, 120,140 of these students hailed from countries within the European Union, while a staggering 559,825 travelled from nations outside the EU to study in the UK. Overall, international students made up nearly a quarter (24%) of the total student population in UK higher education for 2021/22. That's a significant portion! Where did most of these students come from? China topped the list, accounting for 26% of all international students. India came in a close second at 23%, followed by Nigeria at 9%. The UK government had set an ambitious target of hosting at least 600,000 international students per year by 2030. Impressively, that goal was already met in 2020/21 with 605,130 international students. The influx continued in 2022 when a record 484,000 student visas were granted, though the numbers dipped slightly by 5% in 2023. Clearly, the UK remains an extremely attractive study destination for students globally. The diversity of cultures and perspectives these international students bring enriches the academic experience for all. (https://commonslibrary.parliament.uk/research-briefings/cbp-7976/)

For Commonwealth individuals who come to the UK to serve the Crown however, the experience is not the same. One would think that coming all the way to Britain and serving in the British Army would give someone more options to get a better education. Unfortunately, the British military have historically always focused on recruiting soldiers from the low-income families in the North. This practice has deep roots in socioeconomic factors, regional targeting strategies, and historical patterns, all of which have shaped the Army's recruitment policies over time. One of the primary reasons the British Army has focused on recruiting from low-income families is the socioeconomic landscape of these regions. Young people from poorer, working-class backgrounds often face limited economic opportunities. The Army sees these individuals as easier recruits because they may have fewer career prospects and are more likely to be swayed by the promise of stable employment, training, and a sense of belonging. An internal Army document revealed that recruitment efforts specifically targeted 16–24-year-olds from the lowest socioeconomic groups, classified as C2DE. This demographic is perceived as more susceptible to the Army's messaging, which emphasises adventure, camaraderie and personal development. This focus on recruiting from disadvantaged backgrounds isn't new. The Army has a long history of drawing recruits from areas with lower educational attainment and higher poverty levels. This trend suggests that the military has always relied on these communities to fill its ranks. The economic conditions in these regions make military service an attractive option for many young people looking for stability and opportunity. So naturally, when the British military recruit Commonwealth individuals, they expect the same mentality from them. In fact, I would also argue that the country as a whole sees soldiers as uneducated people with ranks. Officers, on the other hand,. traditionally come from a middle class family and would have a further education after college. But there are fewer officers than soldiers. At the time of my writing this book in 2024, Britain has fewer soldiers than the Napoleonic era and the Government is thinking of bringing back national service.

The sun had barely peeked over the horizon when Seru stepped onto the weathered dock of his small village on Vanua Levu. The salty breeze ruffled his dark hair as he joined a small crowd of fellow islanders waiting for the ferry. This wasn't just a leisurely trip – for Seru and many others, the boat was their lifeline to work, school, and essential services on larger islands. As the aging vessel appeared in the distance, Seru adjusted his backpack filled with produce from his family's farm to sell at the market in Suva. This weekly journey was crucial for many in his community, connecting their remote island to the bustling capital on Viti Levu. This was the daily routine for Seru in Fiji, with over 300 islands, this was one of the best ways to commute – I have not yet been to Fiji, but it is high on my to-do list.

So, naturally with this background, Seru choose a career working with boats when he enlisted in the British Army during their mass recruitment drive in Fiji in 2003. Ben's story is not unique. Every year, around 13,000 soldiers transition to civilian life, with approximately 400 of them being Commonwealth veterans. As we discussed his experiences, Ben shared a common frustration among many veterans: "They won't accept me for a degree because my A levels are from Fiji," he explained. Despite his extensive experience as a marine engineer, including work on major container liners, Ben found himself facing unexpected barriers to higher education in the UK. One institution even required Ben to retake his A levels in the UK. However, when the Covid-

19 pandemic hit, it derailed his plans, leaving him feeling discouraged about his prospects for further education.

This situation highlights a significant challenge faced by many Commonwealth veterans – despite having accumulated years of valuable work experience, they often struggle to access higher education opportunities that could facilitate their transition to civilian careers. The contrast is stark: while some Commonwealth veterans with over 15 years of experience find themselves unable to access higher education, their first-born children are heading off to university to start their undergraduate degrees. This disparity underscores the unique challenges faced by mid-career veterans transitioning to civilian life, compared to younger veterans or traditional students. At Leavers to Leaders, we've made it our mission to address this issue. We encourage our participants to leverage their extensive work experience to gain further education and transition into better roles. We recognise that while job-hopping every two years might be beneficial for a 20-year-old gaining experience, for a mid-career professional with 15 years' experience, stability and specialisation become more crucial. Ben's story serves as a poignant reminder of the complexities involved in transitioning from military to civilian life, especially for Commonwealth veterans. It highlights the need for more flexible and inclusive pathways to higher education and career advancement for these individuals who have served and made sacrifices for the UK.

Perhaps the biggest challenge is the fact that English is not our mother tongue. Yet many Commonwealth individuals can write better English than their British counterparts because growing up under the Empire and Commonwealth, English has been well taught in most countries. Take Zimbabwe for example, most of its citizens are very well educated. The first challenge is that higher education institutions in Britain still think that the standard from the Commonwealth is lower and refuse to accept the certificates from overseas. Take, for example, Mat who came to the UK with a degree from Ghana and was only allowed to join as a soldier. 'I was more qualified on paper and in practise than my Major in the Royal Engineers and he knew about that,' Mat explained when I spoke with him. 'Engineering has always been something I always enjoyed back home.' Matt entered the UK with a Master's Degree but was only given an offer to become a soldier and not an officer. Although he ended up enjoying his career as a soldier, he only did seven years and left to join the private sector. This was not a smooth transition either. He had to once again prove his competency, allow people to get more comfortable with him, and perhaps the most challenging was his Ghanaian accent. After moving three to five jobs in the last of three years, he decided that Britain was not for him and returned to Ghana.

Today, when we work with similar learners like Mat, we first align them with a mentor who is not just familiar with diversity and inclusivity, but understands the reason why Commonwealth individuals like Mat are in the UK. Last week, the Government published an article in the national press on the Reserves' liability for callout and a revealed that a staggering 70,000 veterans can be recalled for reserve service. Perhaps what they didn't realise is that some people may not even be in the UK. Once again, this shows how Britain has not taken care of its Commonwealth veterans and neglected the unique way of further developing them as ambassadors who can be a force for positive change around the world, something which is our core focus in the LTL Academy.

Chapter Sixteen

Employment for Commonwealth

I often see career expos and career agencies pitch to Commonwealth personnel in the same way as they would if they were marketing to the guy next door. Depending on the experience within the forces, a Commonwealth person is always wary when encountering the services of a British person. Why is that? For one, this is seen as a business transaction; for two, they more than likely have had an off-putting experience in the past and are therefore suspicious of the prejudices of others. Regardless of the era they arrived in the UK, outside their uniforms they are seen as the typical guy who 'came off the boat'. Many people do not realise that we are judged by our appearance, the colour of our skin, our accent and unfortunately our names.

Early this year, I met with a Nigerian veteran who had been looking for a job for 6 months. He had been out of the Forces for 12 months. His first job lasted six months and his wife was expecting a second child. He came to the career fair which was very well organised by the team at the British Forces Resettlement Service (BFRS). His first words when seeing me were: 'Man, you are so right about career transition; I wish I had taken your advice. I sometimes feel people are judging me by my name before they even give me a chance.' This was perhaps true, but I saw these as words of desperation. He then proceeded to show me how many emails he had sent in the last week – there were a lot, but not one of the recipients had replied to him. Another veteran, this time from Kenya, decided to change his first name to a Christian name so that he could be interviewed and be in front of the person to pitch his skills. This is probably going to resonate with many of my Commonwealth colleagues.

We already know that Commonwealth veterans in the UK who are part of the global majority face an uphill battle when it comes to employment. A report by Professor Mark Williams, led by the Institute of Social and Economic Research, shows that they often earn less than their White counterparts and are twice as likely to be stuck in insecure zero-hour contracts or have to work at short notice. The poorer average labour market prospects of certain Black, Asian, and Minority Ethnic (BAME) groups compared with their White or White British counterparts in the United Kingdom (UK) is well-documented. From my years of experience working with Commonwealth individuals from a wide range of countries across a wide spectrum of people, their individual experience in the labour market will vary from region to region.

Many Commonwealth veterans forget that they will always be a second choice when it comes to the picking order for work, which is a very disturbing reality in the UK. The study Outcomes in Labour Market for Ethnic Minorities by Immigrant Generation Status of 2023 examined the working age adults of ethnic minorities by immigrant generations living in the UK. This research looked at how well different groups of working-age adults (aged 16 to 64) in the UK were faring in the job market, comparing first-generation immigrants (born outside the UK), second-generation immigrants (with at least one parent born outside the UK), and White British people (whose parents were both born in the UK). While some ethnic minority groups see better employment rates and lower economic inactivity among second-generation immigrants compared to White British people, other ethnic groups still face disparities, with higher unemployment and inactivity rates. After accounting for factors like education, health, marital status, location, English proficiency, and having young children, the study found that education and health are the biggest determinants of employment outcomes. Additionally, being single is linked to higher unemployment for men, while having a child under 16 is associated with higher economic inactivity for women.

Crucially, a person's immigrant generation plays a vital role in shaping employment prospects for ethnic minorities in the UK.

I remember talking with Vincent who was leaving the Army as a Captain after 27 years; he was promoted to a Late Entry Officer and extended his service for another 5 years. At 50, Caribbean-born with a very polished Caribbean accent, he said to me: 'I know I am not a corporate type.' He was probably right as even though he has been in the UK for that long, he still has his strong Caribbean accent. So many Commonwealth veterans end up in casual work and self-employment – not out of choice, but due to barriers shutting them out of traditional jobs. For those born outside the UK, the pay gaps are even wider. But job quality isn't just about the pay cheque and security. There's an overlooked aspect that hasn't received much research attention until now – the level of autonomy and control Commonwealth individuals have over their daily tasks and how to approach them. In a first of its kind, large-scale UK analysis, researchers took a deeper look at this "job control" factor across different ethnic groups. What they found reveals some stark divides. While Chinese and Indian minorities are more likely to land professional and managerial roles with higher autonomy, their Pakistani, Bangladeshi, Black African and Black Caribbean counterparts face the opposite reality. These groups are overrepresented in routine and manual labour jobs with very little control over their day-to-day work. So you see, the employment playing field isn't just uneven when it comes to wages and job security for Commonwealth individuals. Even those who manage to get hired often find themselves in roles with less autonomy, creativity and task ownership compared to their White peers in similar occupations. It's a nuanced look at job quality that goes beyond just salaries, and highlights another dimension of inequality persisting in UK workplaces. As we strive for a fairer, more inclusive workforce, giving ethnic minorities more control and agency in their work is another critical piece of the puzzle.

(https://www.understandingsociety.ac.uk/blog/2024/01/08/ethnic-minorities-experience-lower-job-quality/)

In May, during my roadshow in the Midlands, I stopped by the HQ of BRFS. Although I know the team well, it was so rewarding to be able to give them a presentation of what life can be like for a Commonwealth veteran when they get lost in transition. James the Operations Manager and Neil the Director were both very accommodating. I left their office with a positive feeling that morning. If every organisation had taken the time to fully understand Commonwealth soldiers, we would not be in that mess where, for many key organisations, a Commonwealth individual is simply another foreigner, Non-UK, and a migrant. Unfortunately the latest political agenda to stop illegal migrants from entering the UK was not very well handled by the Conservative Government and I am not so sure the Labour Government will handle this any better. Britain removing itself from EU without a plan has now made it impossible for any Brits to work abroad freely or for Europeans to come and work in the UK. 75% of Commonwealth individuals I meet are working either in a low-end job or on a minimum wage after the military. Some who are earning good income have never faced the commercial world but hide within defence organisations. I get it when I meet people in Defence; this is perhaps the best way to be valued for our expertise without having to do any hard-selling. The thing is: if you have ten to fifteen years left to work, then at some point you will have a career transition. However, unless you take charge, you may have little control of your direction. It is like being the driver of your career but with someone else in the driving seat; you will always be in the passenger seat. I once had to explain to my 9-year-old daughter what discrimination looks like so she could better understand it:

'Imagine you and your friend both really want to get hired for a job at the local ice cream shop. Every kids' dream! You both love ice cream and know a lot about the different flavours. You're both really good at scooping ice cream neatly into cones too – which is something we do at home. However, when you go to apply, the owner of the shop looks at you and your friend and decides they only want to hire your friend, not you. This happens even though you're equally good at all the ice cream scooping skills. The only difference is that your friend has blonde hair and you have black hair. That's not fair, is it? She was upset already! The owner is discriminating against you just because of what you look like, not because of how good you'd be at the job. Discrimination means treating someone unfairly or not giving them opportunities, just because of things like their race, religion, gender, disability or age. In the real world, some employers discriminate when hiring people or giving them important jobs, even if those people have all the right skills and experience. They make decisions based on wrong assumptions about what someone can or can't do, just because of how they look or where they came from.'

I hope I did a good job explaining to my daughter. However, discrimination for Commonwealth individuals when searching for work varies according to where they come from. I found that Ghanaians and Nigerians have less problem getting their foot in the door; those from east Africa are more likely to occupy managerial and professional jobs relative to the White British majority; whereas Caribbean and Fijians, and even Gurkhas, are more likely to occupy routine and manual jobs, which also means they are more likely to be replaced by automation.

In 2021, I approached Kul Mahay who was a former Deputy Chief Superintendent of Derbyshire Constabulary to support me and Professor Martin Levermore on a project called 'The D.R.I.V.E Initiative'. The project is about diversity, race, inclusivity, versatility and equality for 15 to 25-year-olds to understand the prospect of life in uniform across the British Army, Royal Air Force, Royal Navy, Fire & Rescue, Ambulance, Prison and Police. The project was well supported by the West Midlands Combined Authority, Birmingham City

University offered us its grounds, and over 250 students from the minority ethnic groups attended. Most of them had never been exposed to people from their own communities and background. We had the parents joining on the final day because we know they are the gatekeepers for each child. The event was so successful that it was on national BBC News that day. This gave us more time to engage with the relevant force and also understand how they operate from the inside. What we both discovered is that many organisations want to bring more representation but do not spend time and investment to prepare their existing team. As a result, they lose their candidates withing a few months. It is like putting new fish into a dirty pond; sooner or later, the new fish will die. Many Commonwealth individuals face constant prejudice while in the military – after all, the military is predominately White which is a fine representation of the country. Currently the White British ethnic group remains the largest at 74.4% of the population. England and Wales have become increasingly diverse over the past decade. This means 24.6% are non-White British from Asian backgrounds, Black African and Caribbean, other mixed ethnic backgrounds including Irish and Arabs. The ethnic diversity is particularly pronounced in major cities that are true melting pots – only 36.8% identified as White British in London, with similar demographics in Leicester (33%) and Birmingham (43%). So while England and Wales remain predominantly White British overall, they have become rich tapestries reflecting peoples from all over the world, especially in the urban centres redefining national identities.

So, how can we as a nation better integrate Commonwealth veterans who travel to the UK, and pay for their rights to become British citizens after their service? The answer is simple: give them a job. By having a job, a Commonwealth individual is able to support his family not just in the UK, but also those back home. My conversation with Inia, a former Fijian Commonwealth veteran who served for 15 years with the Rifles, was a difficult one when he told me: 'People do not realise how hard it can be for us Commonwealth. For two years in a row, we were not able to celebrate Christmas as we had no money to buy foods for the house.' The year after, he worked so hard to make sure this did not happen again. But he told me: "Every two years, I have to find £2,800 just to renew my wife's leave to remain visa.' I cannot believe these things are happening to us. Luckily, my children were born in the UK while I was serving. As I dad myself, I find it painful to hear of children and families struggling to live on minimum wages – especially when Britain is supposed to be a first world country.

Chapter Seventeen

School and Childcare

For the last 18 years or so, I have been lucky to be able to see my daughters heading to school every day and meet some of the other parents in the school playground. While this can be seen as a privilege because many parents cannot actually drive their children to school every day in other countries, in the UK it is a very traditional thing to do. I especially like it when I see grandparents taking on this duty and eavesdrop on the child-friendly conversations they have on the way.

For those of us from the Commonwealth, this family support is not always available. In fact, because most soldiers have served away from their local towns and are likely to have been posted anywhere around the UK, many families do not have access to immediate extended family support. During my quest to uncover the Commonwealth Experience, I met with a Jude and Jack who came from Kenya to join the British Army. Like me, Jack was recruited from the UK and has three beautiful daughters. 'My first daughter was due in 2003, and I was told that I was getting deployed to Op Telic when my wife was four months pregnant. My staff sergeant was a very grumpy person, the type of person who makes you feel very uncomfortable to speak with and I was always avoiding her. She was always in a not-so-good mood – whenever she entered a room, everyone went silent. I was a young private; I always felt they were talking about me each time after I left the room. In the army, it can be like that and it is easy to be pushed in a corner or get left out in a shed, especially if you are in a small unit. Before I left, we were trying to bring my mother-in-law over to the UK to assist my wife before the baby arrived; she did not drive. That was a huge problem.' This is where all the issues started, he explained. Coming from Kenya, one has to apply for a visiting visa prior to entering the UK. 'We were living in a Married Quarters and in 2003, no one fully understood the Service Family Accommodation (SFA) rules.' These Tri-service accommodation regulations (TSARs) are written in such a way that no soldier would understand them. But from reading the lines, the rules say that visitors are permitted to stay on a temporary basis for no more than 28 days (aggregated or continuous) in any 93-day period unless previously authorised. This meant Jack would need to go through his chain of command to get permission to have his mother-in-law staying at his house over a longer period. But first, he had to save the money to apply for the visa, then the flight, and also prove that he had sufficient money in the bank to support his mother-in-law. 'I was a private, the lowest rank and pay in the army,' he said. Eventually, he took on some extra work during the weekend, without letting anyone know, to get some extra money. This was all before they sent him to Telic.

Finally, the baby came, he was able to get back from tour and his mother-in-law was staying with them for six months. 'I decided not to let the army know about the extra stay – we were living in fear for five months that someone would evict us from the house. People at my work have never worked with a Commonwealth individual from Kenya before; they didn't want to know anything about my baby. No one ever asked me about how my baby was in the first three months she was born. We were living in a remote camp in the North. I always felt like I was the only Black man in the village.'

The above sentiments are very true for many Commonwealth individuals, but unfortunately it gets harder once you are outside the wire. Most spouses have to be full-time mums or navigate the complexity of army life. As a result, many Commonwealth spouses are not able to full integrate a British life in the UK. Those who are blessed to be surrounded by a community of their own are also stuck in a what I call 'group-think' mentality and this has its benefits and limitations. I see this with Fijians, Gurkhas and the African families. These groups provide a mental support to the families as they deal with some of the prejudices against them with the wire. But I sometimes feel that these groups also prevent families from integrating and fully understanding life in the UK for their spouses. When you are able to work and have a network outside the wire, it helps Commonwealth individuals to start the process of integration and slowly adapt to life in the UK.

In his report from the Race Disparity Unit of the Equality Hub (2023), the Rt Hon Kemi Badenoch examines the labour market outcomes of working-age adults (16 to 64-year-olds) of ethnic minorities by immigrant generations living in the UK. The research shows that first-generation immigrants – in our case, Commonwealth individuals – have more struggles in getting a job due to child care. But he also shows that those first-generation families are better able to support their children – as they do not have any other options. While systems are in place by the Army Welfare Services, and they can be very supportive, it is when leaving the Forces that those families struggle the most.

The reality is that every parent wants their child to be better than them economically. No one would like their children to be exactly like them: doing the same job, earning the same living. This is even more important for Commonwealth people who come to serve and raise a family in the UK, so they can have a better living standard. So, the sacrifices that the families have to endure is after a long period of time for their British-born children. I think the greatest example is of the current Prime Minister, Rishi Sunak, whose parents were first-generation migrants from Kenya and made him the focus of their movement to UK by sending him to the best schools, college and university in the country. After 40 years, he has attained the rank of Prime Minister – I cannot see any other position higher than this in the UK. As I write this chapter, the country is preparing for the next general election and those from the Commonwealth are also going to have chance to have their say on who will be the next government. I think winning or losing, Rishi Sunak has set a remarkable achievement in the history of the Commonwealth and this will be something that generations of immigrants and Commonwealth individuals will be talking about at school.

Chapter Eighteen

Justice System

In a small coastal town, a heartbreaking discovery shook the community. A jogger stumbled upon a newborn baby, wrapped in a thin blanket, abandoned near a dense woodland. This tragic find led to a complex and emotionally charged case that would soon unfold in the local courthouse. The baby's mother, Silipa, a 38-year-old woman originally from a neighbouring country, was eventually identified and charged. Her story, as it emerged during the trial, painted a picture of a woman trapped in desperate circumstances. Silipa had arrived in the country with her husband, a former Commonwealth soldier who had served in the British Army until a few years prior. Like many Commonwealth families, they faced numerous challenges that included paying visa fees, relocation, finding a new job and paying for rent. If one thing in this chain of events failed, it would automatically affect the others, adding more pressure on the whole family.

By the time of the incident, the family had lost their right to remain in the country, were receiving no social benefits, and were living in a cramped motel room with their children. When Silipa discovered she was pregnant again, she felt overwhelmed and sought help. However, she was already beyond the point where certain options were available. In the months that followed, she withdrew from medical and social services, hiding her pregnancy even from her husband. On that fateful day, Silipa left her motel room in the early hours, gave birth alone in a secluded area, and then made the devastating decision to leave her newborn daughter near the woodland. The baby, later was discovered dead. During the trial, Silipa's defence painted a picture of a vulnerable woman suffering from acute stress and anxiety, describing her action as "an act of desperation." Despite the sympathy her situation evoked, the jury found Silipa guilty of child abandonment. The judge, while acknowledging her difficult circumstances, sentenced her to a minimum term of nine years in prison. As I wrote about the sentencing, I found myself grappling with the complexity of the situation – the tragedy of an innocent life put at risk and the desperation that drove a mother to such an unthinkable act. This case brought to light the challenges faced by some immigrant families, particularly those who have lost their right to remain. It raised questions about access to support services, mental health care, and the pressures faced by vulnerable individuals in our society. The lead investigator's words after the sentencing stuck with me. He emphasised the importance of reaching out for help, urging expectant mothers in difficult circumstances to seek assistance. His message – that there is always help available, no matter how desperate the situation may seem – felt both hopeful and heartbreaking in the context of this tragedy.

The story you just read leaves out facts that happened in reality. I really wish this could have had a better ending as I served with this guy and know the family. However, in this case, only a multi-agency approach could have resulted in a better outcome. This would mean a joint effort from school, Social Services, community support officers, NHS and immigration services.

Another terrible experience is that of Joram Nechironga, a British Army veteran, who is currently living in a state of perpetual anxiety, battling the threat of deportation to Zimbabwe. His distressing journey began over two decades ago when he moved to the UK. In August 2007, he was granted indefinite leave to remain, a milestone that allowed him to build a life in Britain. He served in the British Army, including a tour in Iraq, and has since considered the UK his home. However, despite his service and long-standing ties to the country, Joram now faces the prospect of being forcibly removed to Zimbabwe, a place where he no longer has any connections. The trouble began when Joram was convicted of a crime four years ago while suffering from untreated PTSD after serving on the frontline. Although he has served his sentence, the conviction triggered a deportation order from the Home Office. On 17 February 2022, he was detained, and his appeal against the deportation order was dismissed, leaving him in a precarious situation. Joram's fear is palpable: "I'm living in fear every second," he says. The thought of returning to Zimbabwe fills him with dread, as he believes his life would be in danger there. On a visit to Zimbabwe in 2006, Mr Nechironga was accused of being a British spy and tortured after officials found his British Army ID. He was told never to return, and believes he faces imminent death if he is sent there according to an interview in the Coventry Telegraph.

"I'm suffering for my service to the country I love," he laments, feeling a profound sense of betrayal and hopelessness. The community in Coventry, where Joram resides, has rallied around him. Local MPs and advocates have made pleas on his behalf, highlighting the injustice of deporting a man who has given so much to the UK. They argue that Joram's service and the life he has built in Britain should count for something and that deporting him would be a grave injustice. Despite the support, the Home Office remains unmoved. Joram's case underscores the harsh realities faced by many Commonwealth veterans who, despite their service, find themselves vulnerable to deportation due to past convictions. It raises crucial questions about the treatment of those who have served the country and the support systems in place for veterans. As Joram continues to fight for his right to stay in the UK, he lives each day with the looming threat of deportation.

As someone deeply invested in the welfare of our veterans, particularly those from Commonwealth countries, I've been following the development of support services with keen interest. Today, I want to shine a spotlight on an organisation that's making waves in veteran support: Op NOVA. Set up by the Forces Employment Charity, Op NOVA is a groundbreaking initiative that supports veterans who have found themselves entangled in the justice system. This service, in my opinion, is long overdue and fills a critical gap in veteran support.

So what makes Op NOVA special? For starters, it's not just about legal aid. The programme takes a holistic approach, offering practical and emotional support across a wide range of areas. From mental health and wellbeing to housing and employment, Op NOVA aims to address the root causes that may have led veterans to offend in the first place. One aspect that particularly excites me is Op NOVA's potential to become an integral part of Op Belonging. For those unfamiliar, Op Belonging is a broader initiative aimed at ensuring no Commonwealth veteran is left without support. The synergy between these two programmes could be transformative. Consider this: many Commonwealth veterans face unique challenges when transitioning to civilian life in the UK. Cultural differences, visa issues, and a lack of local support networks can exacerbate the already difficult process of reintegration. When these challenges lead to brushes with the law, the consequences can be devastating. This is where Op NOVA steps in. Their team, comprised of ex-service personnel and those with experience in the justice system, is uniquely positioned to understand and address these complex issues. They can provide the culturally sensitive, specialised support that Commonwealth veterans desperately need. The statistics speak for themselves.

Since 2014, Op NOVA has worked with over 5,000 veterans according to their website. (https://www.forcesemployment.org.uk/programmes/op-nova/).

An impressive 81% of these veterans reported improved mental health and wellbeing after engaging with the programme. These numbers give me hope. As we move forward, my vision is to see Op NOVA and Op

Belonging working hand in hand, creating a safety net so robust that no Commonwealth veteran falls through the cracks. Whether it's preventing offences through early intervention or providing support post-custody, these programmes have the potential to change lives. In conclusion, while there's still work to be done, the existence of Op NOVA is a significant step in the right direction. It's a testament to our commitment to those who've served – regardless of their background or current circumstances. After all, those who have made sacrifices for our country deserve nothing less.

Chapter Nineteen

Non-UK Veteran and Non-UK Personnel

The 2000s era, from 2001 to 2013, was a time of peak recruitment for the British military. The British Armed Forces needed more people to join the Army, Navy and RAF and the majority of recruitment for the Black, Asians and Minority Ethnics was done by opening the door for Commonwealth individuals to join. Inviting the Commonwealth to join is almost like a tap you have in your kitchen: turn the tap and water comes out. At this time, UK foreign policies were still hostile towards Commonwealth individuals joining the Forces. I was one of those who came off the tap. But overall, Britain was really struggling in keeping up with the demand and supply of labour across the country as we read in Part One. Most of us who joined were from overseas or in the UK, joining on the promise of being part of the UK personnel as a Commonwealth citizen.

This is not the first time Commonwealth individuals became part of the British personnel and served on a parallel with their UK counterparts. The term to describe us during WW1 was Dominion (also, described as non-Britons), then the term became Empire soldiers, then Commonwealth soldiers and now Non-UK personnel. As you can see, the labelling has had a 360-degrees change.

The majority of my batch are from Generation X (born between 1965 to 1980). This is the generation born after baby boomers who were born when the first electronics came to be invented alongside nuclear technologies. So they were the first generation to listen to Walkmans, stereo tapes, Hi-Fi systems, and later in the 80s experience Sky TV. They were clearly earmarked to be the successor leaders in the workplace, though this is not always the case in many industries.

Perhaps the last time we had such a mass recruitment was when Caribbean people came to serve. Approximately 16,000 Caribbean men and women volunteered to serve in the British Armed Forces during WW2, motivated to contribute to the war effort and aid Britain. Caribbean people served in various capacities during the War, including the Women's Auxiliary Air Force (WAAF), Auxiliary Territorial Service (ATS), war factories, forestry, and the Merchant Navy. After the War ended, around 3,000 service personnel from the Caribbean remained in the UK, forming a foundation for the Windrush generation. Many of the Windrush arrivals, such as Sam King (who later became the first Black Mayor of Southwark), were former servicemen seeking new opportunities in Britain after serving during WW2. So, in summary, a significant number of the Windrush migrants had served Britain loyally in the Armed Forces and other wartime roles during WW2, which paved the way for their subsequent migration to help rebuild post-War Britain.

Late in 2023, I came across a new label across the British Armed Forces which really was confusing at first but, after carefully looking in this new label, I came to realise that the terms Foreign and Commonwealth were being removed across most recruitment platforms and being replaced with the term 'Non-UK'. Looking more deeply into how this label is being appropriated, it is very clear it is directed at people like myself who are not UK-born, calling us Non UK personnel and veterans. To this day, I have kept my Allegiance to Crown and Country as I have remained voluntarily in the Regular Reserve since 2007. Now, I am classified as Non-UK personnel and those who served alongside me are called Non-UK veterans. When I speak about this even today, many Commonwealth individuals are not even aware of it – especially those who joined 20 years ago and were able to apply for naturalisation after serving 5 years, which was not an option during my service. This is something I have covered more deeply in my Chapter Seven on Indefinite Leave to Remain. So, even though this cohort are clearly

British citizens and living in the UK, because they joined and served under the Immigration Act 1971, they are classified as Non-UK. This is not 1948 when prejudice and racism was at its peak in Britain, but 2023. This is an era that has suffered from the frozen economy of Covid-19 followed by a rise in the cost of living. Prior to that, the Brexit Referendum in 2016 has been a major destabilising factor in British politics, leading to an unprecedented turnover of prime ministers in a short span of time. So, in roughly 6.5 years since the Brexit vote, the UK has seen five different prime ministers take office, making it the highest turnover in a century across the 54 Commonwealth countries of which UK is a member state. This revolving door of leadership is described as highly unusual for a country once known for stable governance.

The label Non-UK was not widely used in 2023: although the Army has been quietly developing it, it was not used or referred to as a known terminology. While writing of this book, I read several books, including 'Small Island' by Andrea Levy in which she describes how the Caribbean soldiers who came back to Britain faced a different challenge when they actually lived in the UK alongside their British counterparts. For those in the RAF, they soon realised once they took blue uniforms off, they were unable to blend into the tapestry of the UK and, in fact, they faced many prejudices and racism. The story tells us that many found it hard to integrate in British society and had to live in small communities. Today, we are living in a different age. Yet the term Non-UK can be applied to many groups of people who arrived in the UK legally: as economic migrants (like those to replace the skill gap across the various sectors in the UK); illegal migrants and asylum seekers; and those seeking help in the UK like the Afghan veterans. As of December 2023, around 25,000 individuals have arrived in the UK under the Afghan Relocations and Assistance Policy (ARAP) and the Afghan Citizens Resettlement Scheme (ACRS). The UK Government has granted indefinite leave to remain to 12,848 individuals across ARAP and

ACRS pathways as of December 2023. Technically anyone not born in the UK is defined as Non-UK. This label can also be used for the Hong Kong veterans who served while the UK was ruling Hong Kong and are now residing in the UK under the new "Hong Kong Veterans Settlement" that allowed hundreds of Hong Kong nationals who served in the British Armed Forces prior to 1 July 1997 to settle in the UK. Applications for this Hong Kong Veterans Settlement route opened in autumn 2023, following decades of campaigning by former service personnel who were previously denied UK citizenship. This new visa route will enable eligible Hong Kong veterans and their family members (spouse/partner and dependent children) to obtain "indefinite leave to enter" the UK, allowing them to live and work without restrictions. It also provides a potential path to full British citizenship. As I write this book, it is now very official that the British Army is labelling my generation of Commonwealth personnel, who were once known as British Service personnel, as Non-UK personnel and veterans. My question is: why this, why now? How can a country support one cohort who served to defend their own country and disregard another who lived to serve the interest of British citizens in the UK and were all ready to give their lives to the highest authority of Britain? This book is sub-titled, When Did Britain Stop Seeing Us as a Band of Brothers? The more I look into this, the more I ask the question: Were we ever a Band of Brothers? Especially now that we are labelled as 'Non-UK' personnel and veterans.

The struggles for Commonwealth individuals have been widely reported across the media by many newspapers. Many of my counterpart British colleagues know this is unfair and that we should be treated better for service in the homeland and for defending the British anywhere in the world. We have done this alongside many other nationalities like the Gurkhas who joined not to defend their own nations but the interests of Britain. As I write this chapter, veterans who left 10 years ago are still lost in transition and trying to find a way out of the rabbit hole they entered. I have no doubt that this new label is going to have a devastating consequence in the lives of thousands of British Commonwealth veterans across the UK and once again we are seeing ourselves in similar situations as our Windrush brothers and sisters. So my question is: What is the intention behind the label Non-UK for the latest cohort of Commonwealth personnel? Should we really be differentiating between Hong Kong Veterans and Afghan Veterans who protected their own countries and Commonwealth veterans who defended the UK's interest who are living in the UK as veterans?

PART THREE: OP BELONGING

Chapter Twenty
Bula Festival

Every summer, the vibrant spirit of Fiji comes alive in the heart of the UK with the Bula Festival. Originating from Nadi, Fiji, the festival has made its way across continents, bringing with it a celebration of Fijian culture, unity and joy. The word "Bula," (pronounced boo-lah), means "life" in Fijian and is used as a greeting to wish happiness, good health and the energy of life. This essence of Bula is what the festival aims to share with everyone, whether they are from Fiji or any other part of the world. The host is Aldershot, a small garrison military town in the South – also known as the home of the British Army. This was my first time attending this festival as a guest speaker at the invitation of Mr Manoa (who is actually a Reverend) who was our Fijian neighbour back in the days when we were all newly married with no children. As I said before, I had a deep bond in meeting Fijians when I arrived at my first posting in the South. To this day, we always call each other 'Mr Manoa' and he calls me 'Mr Reddy'.

Since it was a Sunday, we arrived around 10.30 that morning. From the moment you stepped into the festival grounds, you were greeted with the warm smiles and enthusiastic "Bula!" from the Fijian community, instantly making you feel part of the family. The festival was a feast for the senses. Traditional Fijian music filled the air, with bands and musicians playing lively tunes that made it impossible not to dance. The rhythmic beats of the Lali drums and harmonious melodies of ukuleles transported you straight to the tropical islands of Fiji. Dancers in vibrant costumes performed the Meke, a traditional dance that tells stories of Fijian ancestors and legends. Food stalls sold dishes like Kokoda (a ceviche of fish marinated in lime juice and coconut), lovo (meats and vegetables cooked in an earth oven), and sweet treats like cassava cake. The aroma of these delicious foods wafted through the air, drawing festivalgoers to sample the rich flavours. Arts and crafts stalls showcased the intricate handiwork of Fijian artisans, from woven mats and baskets to beautifully carved wooden sculptures. These items not only served as souvenirs but also as a testament to the rich cultural heritage of Fiji. This time, the Bula Festival was a three-day celebration of South Pacific culture, transforming the huge football grounds into a vibrant tapestry of tradition and joy.

But the Bula Festival was more than just a celebration of Fijian culture: it showcased the rich diversity of the United Kingdom. Here, you would find communities from all walks of life, particularly those with ties to the defence sector, coming together to share their stories, traditions, and unique perspectives. As you explored the festival, you would find yourself indulging in the tantalising flavours of Fijian cuisine – from the aromatic spices of traditional dishes to the refreshing sweetness of tropical fruits. Each bite would transport you to the sun-drenched shores of the South Pacific.

Perhaps the most captivating aspect of the Bula Festival was the atmosphere itself. It was a place where strangers became friends, where cultural barriers dissolved, and where the spirit soared – whether you were a lifelong resident of Aldershot or a curious traveller seeking new experiences.

The Bula Festival UK was more than just a celebration; it was a bridge between cultures. It brought together Fijians from the 326 islands community and the wider British population, fostering mutual understanding and respect. The festival also served as a platform for charitable causes, with events aimed at raising funds for community projects, educational initiatives and healthcare facilities. For the Fijian diaspora in the UK, the Bula Festival was a cherished tradition that kept them connected to their roots. It provided an opportunity for different generations to come together, pass on cultural knowledge, and ensure the continuation of their traditions for future generations.

I first discovered Fijians in 2002, after completing my training as a Movement Controller in Deepcut and moving into the military pad, also known as married quarters. Although, I met many Africans during my Phase One and Two in Litchfield and Catterick, when Commonwealth soldiers meet each other in the military, there's an unspoken bond of respect and understanding that transcends words. This connection is deeply rooted in shared experiences and a common heritage that dates back generations. It's a bond that has been forged in the heat of battle and the camaraderie of service, much like the soldiers from Commonwealth nations who fought side by side during World War 1 and World War 2. In the modern-day British Army, this bond is evident in the way Commonwealth soldiers interact. As we saw in Part One of this book, we come from diverse backgrounds—Fiji, Ghana, Jamaica, India, and many other nations—but we share a common purpose and a mutual respect. When a Fijian soldier meets a comrade from St. Lucia, there's an immediate recognition of shared struggles and triumphs. They understand the sacrifices each has made to be there, far from home, serving a country that is not their own but has become their new family. It took me a while to fully be able to describe it until I read some of the stories in detention camps.

Sadly as this may sound, or happy as we may look, we as Commonwealth individuals are not that free in the Britain during our service. I have described the horrible atmosphere of being in a room with my Commonwealth and Nepalese folks for a Non-UK personnel brief invented by the British Army five years ago. I do feel for everyone who attended; we should never have been treated that way by the system. It feels so much like the Windrushian treatment that the generation before us endured during their service to the Crown after travelling to the UK. I have covered this topic in Part Two of this book and its impact on the fighting force, retention and recruitment. But at the Bula Festival, this all seemed to be forgotten, everyone was cheerfully greeting and talking with each other with their best South Pacific smiles. However, I also know many Fijians who would prefer not to attend this festival due to their current immigration status.

One that day, I met Tabu who approached me with his wife and his son. Tabu had always been a dedicated soldier, serving in the British Army for 12 years. His career, however, came to a sudden and devastating end when he was dishonourably discharged after allegedly testing positive for drugs. The British Army's strict policies left no room for error and Tabu found himself literally kicked out, his dreams shattered. For a Commonwealth soldier like Tabu, this wasn't just the end of a career. It meant losing his right to stay in the UK. The British Army's values and standards are drilled into every soldier, much like a child learns to read. But for Commonwealth soldiers, the consequences of a discharge can be far more severe. What struck Tabu the most about the British military was its attempt to treat everyone the same. But equality isn't always about identical treatment.

As Abraham Lincoln once said, "If you tell a bird to climb a tree, it will think it is stupid." Similarly, giving a Muslim soldier the same rations as a non-Muslim, when those rations aren't Halal, misses the mark. "We can't expect a Muslim soldier to eat non-halal food any more than we'd expect a fish to climb a tree. It's not about special treatment – it's about allowing each soldier to perform at their best by respecting their needs."

After his discharge, Tabu's life took a turn for the worse. For Commonwealth soldiers, the exemption from immigration control ends

28 days after leaving the services. Without the means to secure his status, Tabu became an illegal immigrant. This was a disgrace not only to him but also to his family and community both in Fiji and the UK. With little savings and no legal right to work, Tabu went underground for ten years. His island community rallied around him, helping him find work where employers didn't check his legal status. He moved from England to Scotland, building connections and scraping by. But everything changed with the new immigration laws introduced by Home Secretary Theresa May. The 2014 Immigration Act made it mandatory for employers to verify the immigration status of their employees, with severe penalties for non-compliance. By 2016, these laws were enforced nationwide, including in Scotland. Tabu could no longer find work, plunging him and his family into destitution. Here was a man who had served 12 years in the British Army, now living in hardship and uncertainty. The Commonwealth dream had turned into a nightmare, trapping him in the UK and unable to travel. The increasingly hostile environment created by these laws has only grown tougher since 2014. Tabu's story is another reminder of the challenges faced by Commonwealth soldiers who serve the King and Crown yet find themselves treated as second-class citizens. Many who have worn the British uniform share this sentiment, feeling the sting of betrayal long after their service has ended. The 2014 Immigration Act, introduced by Theresa May, aimed to create a "hostile environment" for illegal immigrants and many Commonwealth individuals became victims of it – this policy inadvertently affected many members of the Windrush generation who lacked documentation proving their legal status and the third wave of Commonwealth soldiers.

The Act included measures such as requiring private landlords to check the immigration status of tenants, making temporary migrants contribute to the NHS, and mandating banks to verify the immigration status of account holders. These measures were designed to make life difficult for those without legal status, but they also had severe unintended consequences for people like Tabu. For Tabu, the new regulations meant that employers were now legally required to check his immigration status before hiring him. The penalties for non-compliance were steep, with fines of up to £20,000 per illegal worker. This made it nearly impossible for Tabu to find work, as employers were unwilling to take the risk. The law also reduced the grounds for appeal in immigration cases, making it harder for people like Tabu to challenge their status. Theresa May's policies were intended to deter illegal immigration, but they also created a climate of fear and uncertainty for many Commonwealth citizens. The impact on Tabu's life was profound, leaving him trapped in a country for which he had served but now felt alienated from. His story is a powerful example of the unintended consequences of the 2014 Immigration Act and a reminder of the ongoing struggles faced by Commonwealth soldiers in the UK.

Chapter Twenty-One
Commonwealth Commemoration Parade on Black History Month

In my book *Leavers to Leaders*, I shared my childhood dream of being part of something grand rather than being confined to a small, exotic island in Africa, nestled in the Indian Ocean. This island, Mauritius, is a melting pot of cultures—Indian, Chinese, Tamil, Muslim, and African—blended with a French influence but lacking the ideals of liberty, equality, and fraternity. Shocking inequality has plagued the island since the first indentured labourers arrived in 1833. A drive through Tamarin on the West Coast reveals a contrast between the rich and the poor, with affluent people living in luxurious villas overlooking the serene blue ocean. This disparity is evident in the north and east coasts as well. The African descendants, who were once slaves to French planters before the indentured labourers arrived, suffered the most. Some people compare the conditions of indentured labourers to those of slaves, which might be understandable based on historical accounts. However, I believe we cannot equate the lives of these two groups after their emancipation. Although African slaves were freed, they were left with nothing but their freedom on an isolated island—no jobs, no shelter, no clothes, and no food. This ongoing struggle of African and Black people, many of whom still live in slums across Mauritius, including those displaced from Diego Garcia, should concern us all.

On the other hand, indentured labourers had the opportunity to buy or lease land, allowing them to start anew, while African slaves wandered penniless. Britain's efforts to abolish the slave trade significantly impacted other nations. The British Navy enforced the ban by patrolling the West African coast, influencing other colonies around

1833. This historical event, often overlooked, played a crucial role in shaping the world we live in today.

As the autumn leaves began to turn, painting Southampton in warm red and gold hues, I found myself caught in the anticipation of the first day of Black History Month. The year was 2023, and the air was buzzing with excitement for the Commonwealth Commemoration Parade. Two months before, I received a call from Abdoulie, the energetic Chair of United Voice of Africa. His voice crackled with enthusiasm as he shared his latest project – Southampton's first Black Business Arts and Music Festival, affectionately dubbed BBAM. "We need your help," he said, "to invite the Black and Commonwealth soldiers from the British Army. Can you do it?" Without hesitation, I agreed and soon found myself navigating the familiar streets to St. Mary's Community Centre, just behind Royal South Hants Hospital, to meet with him a week later.

As I walked, memories flooded back of my early days in the military, when I'd frequent this area for its authentic African and Asian cuisine. The community centre bustled with activity as Abdoulie and I sat down to plan. The aroma of spices from nearby shops wafted through the open windows, reminding me of the culinary adventures I'd shared with my wife years ago. We used to drive around on festive days, marvelling at the vibrant streets and diverse faces – an iron contrast to our peaceful home in Marchwood, a predominantly White village on the outskirts of the New Forest. As we worked, I found myself reflecting on my journey. Here I was, exactly half my life spent in Britain, the other half in Mauritius. I arrived at 24, a young man full of dreams and uncertainties. Now, mid-career, I realised how much I'd been shaped by British culture – the art of polite conversation, the harmless banter, the subtle dance of social interactions and the small talk that a few years back during the 'ash cloud' got me and two complete strangers stuck in Dubai into a car journey from Manchester to Southampton. As Abdoulie and I finalised our plans for the festival, I felt a sense of belonging. This event, we both knew, was more than just a celebration of culture and heritage; it was a testament to how far we had come and a reminder of the journey ahead. We both arrived in the UK during the same year and in some way this was a huge step for us. As I left the community centre, the setting sun cast long shadows across the street and I smiled, ready to embrace whatever the future held.

Now the challenge was ahead of me, I did what any trained soldier would do. I said 'yes' to an event that was happening right here in the city where I was naturalised and home to my three daughters – perhaps the single most talked about event for Op Belonging.

It is a very sad fact that the involvement of Commonwealth soldiers during both WW1 and WW2 is not well recorded and celebrated. Perhaps if the stories of the 2.5 million people from the Commonwealth were captured, we would have hundreds of books like this one in libraries and archives and stories to share with our children and grandchildren. Perhaps it is because they all served under Britain's colonies which later became known as the Commonwealth. Looking at India, for example, the country of my ancestors: India was the greatest contributor with 1.5 million brave volunteers who came forward to serve in World War 1. Of these, 140,000 Indian troops saw active combat on the brutal Western Front in Europe. Their courage and sacrifices were immense – Indian soldiers won an astounding 13,000 medals, including 12 prestigious Victoria Crosses, for their heroic actions during the War. Some 15,000 soldiers from the West Indies Regiment fought valiantly in France, Palestine, Egypt, and Italy during the First World War. Their service came at a heavy cost, with 2,500 of them killed or wounded on the battlefields. However, their bravery shone through, earning 81 medals for courageous acts, while 49 were mentioned in dispatches for their gallantry. Africa made a vital contribution, with 55,000 men from countries like Nigeria, Gambia, Rhodesia (now Zimbabwe), South Africa, Sierra Leone, Uganda, Nyasaland (now Malawi), Kenya, and the

Gold Coast (now Ghana) fighting for the British. Hundreds of thousands more served as carriers or auxiliaries, playing crucial support roles. Tragically, an estimated 10,000 African soldiers lost their lives, but their sacrifices were recognised with 166 decorations for bravery. In total, over 1,000,000 men from ethnic minorities within the British Empire served in the First World War, making invaluable contributions across multiple fronts and theatres of this global conflict.

When the dark clouds of World War 2 gathered, India was not a self-governed nation. The decision for India to join the War and fight alongside Britain was made in London, as the British Government still held direct rule over the subcontinent. Despite this lack of autonomy, brave Indian volunteers stepped forward in droves to join the British Indian Army. In September 1939, at the outbreak of the War, the British Indian Army had only 250,000 men. However, by the time the conflict ended, a staggering 2.5 million Indian volunteers had joined its ranks, making an immense contribution to the war effort. Their courage and sacrifices were extraordinary, with Indian troops winning 30 prestigious Victoria Cross medals for acts of remarkable bravery. Tragically, 87,000 Indian soldiers paid the ultimate price, losing their lives in service. As India bled for the Allied cause, some voices within the country argued that in return for their unwavering support during the War, they should be granted independence from British rule. However, these aspirations were rejected by the British Government, dashing the hopes of those who had sacrificed so much for a promise of freedom. Despite being drawn into a conflict not of their own making, the Indian people answered the call with remarkable courage and determination. Their sacrifices and contributions during World War 2 were immense, and their valour in the face of adversity remains a testament to their resilience and commitment to the cause of freedom.

As an important maritime port, Southampton played a crucial role in both World Wars. It served as an embarkation point for troops and supplies being sent to the various fronts. Casualties occurring during training, transportation, or other military activities in the area were buried in local cemeteries. During World War 1, many buildings in Southampton were converted into military hospitals to treat wounded and sick soldiers from the Western Front and home front – around New Forest, Winchester and, a few miles from my house, was Netley Hospital which was one of the largest in the South after Brighton.

So when The United Voice of African Associations (TUVAA) invited me to support the first ever festival to celebrate the contribution of Black people in Hampshire, I saw Abdoulie's passion for this initiative. It was not another organisation trying to raise funding or make some noise about Black history. It was deeper than that. We met and spoke on several occasions and it was during those times that I came to understand the passion behind his vision. Abdoulie came to the UK around the same time as me, pursuing his studies while working part-time in the care industry. Even back in those days, although work was readily available (you could quit your job in the morning and by 4pm you could have another job), those jobs were for the lower end of the market. These were jobs for your typical students like cleaners, bartenders, carers, book keepers, warehouse packers and agency drivers.

For a few months I supported Abdoulie on his vision, then I decided that for this event Black Business, Art and Music, we would organise a Commonwealth Commemoration Parade to remember the sacrifices of all Black and Commonwealth soldiers during the Wars. This was the beginning of furthering the mission of Op Belonging. Having a vision and delivering on the vision are two separate things: we all know that ideas and visions are useless without practical plans. But what added fuel to the idea of hosting the first Commonwealth Parade for Black History Month was that Southampton is home to the largest cemetery for the Commonwealth war graves.

In the aftermath of World War 1, the city of Southampton undertook a solemn task – to honour and commemorate the fallen heroes from their community. In November 1918, the Southampton War Memorial Committee began compiling a list of all those from the Borough of Southampton who had made the ultimate sacrifice, with their names to be inscribed on the Borough War Memorial. However, in 1920, the boundaries of the Borough were much smaller than the present-day city. Areas like Bassett, Bitterne, Bitterne Manor, Bitterne Park, Itchen, Midanbury, Millbrook, Peartree Green, Redbridge, Sholing, Swaythling, Thornhill, Weston, and Woolston were not yet part of Southampton. To ensure that no hero was forgotten, these districts erected their own memorials. Bassett Parish established a war memorial, while a larger monument was constructed in the St Mary's Extra cemetery on Portsmouth Road, along the east bank of the River Itchen. This memorial recorded the names of the fallen from the parish of St Mary Extra, which encompassed much of what is now Southampton. Not to be left behind, the Jesus Chapel (Peartree Church) erected its own war memorial in the churchyard at the centre of Peartree Green, honouring the sacrifices of its community. The War Memorial Committee's efforts culminated in the collection of 1,793 names, which were meticulously inscribed onto the recessed faces of the central pylon of Lutyen's Cenotaph, ready for the dedication ceremony. The pamphlet for the ceremony rounded this number up to 1,800 names, suggesting that the committee may have been still collecting names as the publication went to press. (https://www.southampton.gov.uk/arts-heritage/collections-monuments/cenotaph/)

In addition to the war graves, Southampton has several significant memorials commemorating Commonwealth casualties, such as the Hollybrook Memorial and the Southampton Cenotaph. The Hollybrook Memorial alone commemorates nearly 1,900 Commonwealth service members who died in the First World War. Through these memorials, the city of Southampton and its surrounding areas ensured that the sacrifices of their sons and daughters during the Great War would never be forgotten, etching their names into the fabric of the community for generations to come. So, based on this evidence, hosting the first Commonwealth Commemoration Parade was just a beginning for Op Belonging, our social arm at Leavers to Leaders.

Deep down, I saw the vison and impact of an event like this, on the South Coast would mark the beginning of what I called 'building bridges' between organisations, communities, veterans and service personnel. I had very little connection with the key person within the military wire. Earlier that year, I had met with the executives of SASRA, an organisation that had been founded on the principle of supporting those behind the wire with their Christian faith. I have known SASRA (Soldiers, Aviators, Scripture Readers Association) back in 2001 in Catterick Garrison during my Phase Two training with as a Royal Fusilier. Going into their head office in Aldershot, I was hoping would be a step forward. After our talks, it was clear to me that they only focused on people within the wire and were not so interested to support veterans after the military.

One of the key challenges is that organisations sometimes hide behind political language. For example, one organisation said to me: 'We treat everyone equally, Black, White, regardless of their gender or race.' While this has been the stated approach for years in the UK, the lived experiences of those people from a race and ethnic background are often very different as shown by the stories of those shared in this book. I remember reading 'Animal Farm' in secondary school in Mauritius as part of the English literature class. It was perhaps the most fascinating subject because the teacher was very good at making us into characters and explaining the stories almost made you imagine the lives of these animals. A particular line in this book is: 'All animals are equal, but some animals are more equal than others'. This quote has stuck with me forever. Is this what I was hearing: they believe we are actually equal in Britain? Saying that everyone is equal in a predominately majority White country with minority Black, Asian and other ethnic military people, does not sound equal at all. For example, when someone from the Commonwealth departs from the military, the steps required for this person are not the same as for the UK-born personnel. The fear of getting rejected for the indefinite leave to remain or naturalisation is real for thousands who have left and those about to leave. So maybe the quote should be: 'Everyone is equal but some people are less equal than others – so don't treat everyone equally.' Treat them according to the level of need and support they need.

As the autumn leaves began to fall, I found myself embarking on a journey that would reconnect me with old friends and forge new bonds. It all started with a flurry of emails to various army units across the South. After weeks of exchanging emails, my persistence paid off when an invitation arrived from the 17 Port & Maritime Regiment in Southampton, which is part of the Royal Logistics Port, a regiment I knew very well as a young Movement Controller back in 2002.

Upon arrival, I was greeted by a familiar face: Ben, now a Warrant Officer Class One. Memories flooded back of the young Junior Non-Commissioned Officer I'd known 18 years ago. I remembered him well as a quiet but highly effective Junior Non-Commissioned Officer. Seeing his career progression as a Fijian and reaching the pinnacle of his trade as a Port Operator was truly a cause for celebration. I was warmly greeted by several enthusiastic faces, all eager to be part of the first Commonwealth Commemoration Parade. Beside him stood Selorm, a young Ghanaian Warrant Officer whose career had skyrocketed. Little did I know he was set to play a key role in the parade. The Commanding Officer and the Second in Command's email support buoyed my spirits, though I couldn't shake off a nagging disappointment that The Royal Logistics Corps Association's lukewarm response hinted at some unseen resistance to my plans. My vision was to see a good mix of people from all 56 Commonwealth countries. Emailing the regional South-West team proved to be a nightmare. One individual in particular seemed to misunderstand the significance of the parade, viewing it as mediocre, and gave little support. Faced with this resistance, I had no choice but to escalate the matter. I reached out to the Army HQ in Andover and, within a day, my inbox was flooded with responses from across the South West and South East. The responses were overwhelmingly positive, much to the embarrassment of the regional SO1.

As I stepped into the Sergeant's mess at 17 Port & Maritime Regiment, I was enveloped by a sea of friendly Commonwealth faces. We gathered in a spacious living area, the air thick with camaraderie and shared experiences. Ben and I reminisced about old times, while I forged connections with the others. Amidst the lively chatter, a realisation struck me. Two decades ago, many in this room would have been Junior Non-Commissioned Officers, perhaps not even allowed in this mess. Now, they were sitting comfortably, at home within the wire. Yet, I couldn't help but wonder how many truly understood life beyond these familiar confines. As the evening wore on, I marvelled at how far we had all come. The parade plans were taking shape, promising to be a celebration of our shared journey and the progress we had made. But more than that, it was a testament to the bonds forged in service, transcending rank and time.

So, getting a Commemoration Parade together when I am technically outside the wire was a challenge. But the advantage is, that when those who joined with you are actually at the top of their ranks, the task becomes less challenging. As a Movement Controller, I was the first Commonwealth member to step foot in this regiment, a challenge I embraced wholeheartedly. My previous experience running the airport and port operations in Mauritius as a freeport officer had prepared me well for this task – this time without the shirt and tie, but in military combat, ready to organise the shipment of bombs and missiles to major war theatres. The unique perspective and skills I brought from my civilian experience were invaluable in this new role.

However, organising the Commonwealth Parade was just beginning. The parade was more than just an event; it was a celebration of our progress and the bonds we had forged in service and understanding that we are also standing on the shoulders of giants. It was a testament to our resilience and the diverse, vibrant community that has been built since 1919.

The day of finally arrived. I had some pre-planning with the Council and the event organiser on what I wanted the day to look like for the maximum benefit of each and every one in attendance. At 10am that day, everything was ready: the team from 17 arrived on a coach, we had Selorm as Sergeant Major, and this became the highlight of the BBAM festival. Everyone played their part. We were joined by veterans from the British Army and Royal Navy, but I didn't have any contact with the Royal Air Force Network as yet. What made the event even more beautiful was my encounter with Sir Neil Flannagen and his team. Seeing my own daughter doing the MC for this event was a complete success, under the watchful eyes of my brother Michael who has always supported our events with his wife. Michael did us the honour of leading the Commemoration by laying a wreath for all those from the Caribbean who gave their lives in the Wars – he himself has a Caribbean heritage although he was born in London. He is perhaps the first person I know who joined the British Army as a soldier and left as a Lieutenant Colonel. We ended the day with a group photo which you can see on our Facebook page and, as I write this chapter, plans are now in place for the 2nd Commonwealth Commemoration Parade this year.

Chapter Twenty-Two
Black History Month in the British Military

The month of October is the Black History Month across the UK, a tradition that started here in 1987, over a decade after it began in the United States. In the mid-1980s, Akyaaba Addai-Sebo, a Ghanaian activist working as a Special Projects Coordinator for the Greater London Council, was deeply troubled by a concerning trend he observed. "Black children in Britain were facing an identity crisis," he recalled in an interview. "Some would brazenly refuse to identify with Africa and even shrink away when called African." Moved by this disconnect from their roots, Akyaaba joined forces with other passionate community activists, determined to address this issue. Together, they embarked on a mission to celebrate and promote awareness of Black history and heritage in the UK. Their efforts culminated in 1987 when they successfully organised the country's first ever Black History Month celebration in London. This groundbreaking event aimed to reconnect Black British youth with their rich African origins and instil a sense of pride in their cultural identity. (https://www.blackhistorymonth.org.uk/article/section/interviews/akyaaba-addai-sebo/)

The inaugural celebration was a resounding success, sparking a wave of enthusiasm that quickly spread across the nation. Boroughs and communities throughout the UK embraced the initiative, formally recognising October as Black History Month – a time to honour and explore the histories, contributions, and experiences of African, Asian, and Caribbean peoples in Britain's diverse "island story". What began as a grassroots movement to address an identity crisis has since blossomed into a nationwide celebration, a testament to the power of community activism and the enduring importance of embracing one's roots. Black History Month in the UK now stands as a vibrant platform for fostering understanding, appreciation and unity among all Britons, regardless of their backgrounds. This was a pivotal moment for Britain, one which cannot be overlooked anymore. As we saw in Part One, the free movement of Commonwealth nations started way before 1944 and it took over 40 years to have such a celebration spread out across Britain. Today, it is amazing to see council leaders all over planning an event to mark the significance of this month. However, my observation is that across the British military, this is much less celebrated. After organising the Commonwealth Commemoration Parade during Black History Month, I spoke to those who attended about their local regimental plan for Black History Month and was surprised to note that many had no plans. Admittedly, the Army and Navy are probably at their busiest since last year, with more commitments around the world and less people to deploy. But even if they had 10 people on site, an event like this deserves to be celebrated.

It was with this idea in mind that I visited two Army regiments, one in the South in Bicester and the other one in Cheshire, to encourage them to celebrate the diversity of the Army. On the first visit to 1 Regiment Royal Logistic Corps, I was delighted to have Abdoulie with me – he and I previously collaborated to organise the BBAM festival in Southampton. The turnout was great, we had over 90 people from various African and Caribbean countries attending. I spoke about career mapping for those thinking of leaving and Abdoulie spoke about diversity. I could see in the eyes of all those attending that they really valued this moment together and it meant something to them. What was also encouraging was to see many British soldiers also joining this event. The British Army, like many other institutions, has recognised the importance of fostering a sense of belonging and inclusivity for all its members, regardless of their cultural backgrounds. To this end, the Army has established its own Multicultural Network, an initiative that aims to celebrate diversity and promote a culture of acceptance within its ranks. However, as Michael, a Black soldier born in the UK, can attest, the journey towards true belonging has been a long and arduous one. Despite serving a full term and being promoted to the rank of Lieutenant Colonel – a remarkable achievement as the first officer of mixed heritage to reach this milestone – his experiences as a Black soldier in the 1980s were far from ideal. In a recent conversation, Michael recalled the harrowing times when his White colleagues attempted to set him on fire on multiple occasions. Faced with blatant racism and discrimination, he recalled how as a child he had resorted to trying to scrub away his skin colour in the bathtub – a heartbreaking testament to the psychological toll of such mistreatment. Yet, through it all, Michael persevered, his unwavering determination propelling him to the highest echelons of the Army's ranks, paving the way for future generations of officers from diverse backgrounds.

While progress has been made, there is still work to be done to ensure that every individual, regardless of their race or ethnicity, feels truly valued and accepted within these organisations. Initiatives like Black History Month serve as powerful reminders of the rich tapestry of cultures that have contributed to the fabric of British society, and the importance of celebrating and embracing this diversity. This year, the Black History Month festival in Southampton promises to be a particularly significant event, with the theme of "Op Belonging" aiming to raise awareness and foster a sense of inclusivity within a one-hour radius of the city. The goal is to ensure that every regiment has a place at the festival, a symbolic gesture that underscores the Army's commitment to embracing and celebrating the diverse backgrounds of its members. As Akyaaba Addai-Sebo's pioneering efforts demonstrated, celebrating cultural heritage is not just about acknowledging the past; it is about paving the way for a future where everyone, regardless of their background, can feel a true sense of belonging and acceptance within the institutions they serve.

Chapter Twenty-Three

Fiji Day

Last year, I was invited to speak at Fiji Day in Dreghorn Barracks in Edinburgh. Fiji Day is celebrated on the 10 October in the UK to commemorate two key events in Fiji's history – the ceding of Fiji to the United Kingdom in 1874 and Fiji gaining independence from British rule in 1970. Fiji Day is commemorated in the UK primarily by the Fijian community and British military regiments with longstanding ties to the island nation, celebrating its independence from British colonial rule.

The journey from Southampton to Edinburgh is straightforward by plane, but this time I wanted to make a road trip out of it and visited a few barracks on my way. Since Fiji Day falls in Black History Month as well, I stopped in the Midlands and Catterick, before arriving in Dundee at the Invercarse Hotel which is set right across from the small airport and on the River Tay. This was not my first time in this hotel – it is a very contemporary venue which we have been using for all our corporate training and career workshops with clients. Arriving at midnight and having a shower after a 12-hour drive was very welcoming before bed. The next day was going to be full-on.

I started my day with my usual video call with my wife and daughters at 8am just before they set off for school. It is a daily routine that I have established. Then at 9am, my brother Alaa came to have breakfast with me. By now, you will realise that if I respect someone dearly I will always greet them as 'brother' which is 'frero' in Creole. When I first met Alaa on a Zoom call, I knew we had an instant connection. I know a lot about Egypt as a Christian and reading Moses, but what really connected us was our passion for our cultures. His dad was an officer in the Egyptian Army so he also understood my line of work well. An even greater symbolical connection between us was that my grandfather Murday T. Reddy served in Egypt during WW2; his name is in one of the museums in Egypt. Alaa and I both have a passion for developing leaders and have both written amazing books about it.

At 11am, we went to visit his new venture where he is the CEO of Dundee Business Centre of Excellence and met with his team and had lunch at the V&A in Dundee – Scotland's design museum set by the side of the River Tay, overlooking Tayside and the bridge linking the two places. It is a really wonderful setting if you visit Dundee. Then, I left for the Royal Scots Regiment in Dreghorn Barracks where the Rifles and a few other regiments are located for Fiji Day and met with Mo and his wife for the second time. The last time we met was at the Bula Festival in Aldershot.

It was after my speech that I met Iveri. He thanked me for my talk on standing out and after a few minutes introduced me to his son. He was a well-built man already in his mid-twenties and it was then that we struck a connection – he was a family man. Iveri has since joined our Foundation Programme and is now completing his Accelerator in Leavers to Leaders in the care industry. Iveri is perhaps the first Fijian to become a care home manager in the UK – an industry I am very familiar with having owned and run my own care homes as my second career after the military. He is from Lawaki village in Kadavu Province, which has a traditional hierarchy of chiefs from southern and western Fiji, and is about 80 km south of Suva (the capital city) by sea. From my understanding, this island is well-known for sending the best teachers, lawyers and engineers around Fiji. Iveri has this natural deep-voice resonance and tone which I think must have made all his students very respectful of him.

His childhood on the island makes you think of Huckleberry Finn in the famous novel by Mark Twain which was first published in 1884. The story begins when Huck's father comes back to town, kidnapping him and taking him to a cabin across the Mississippi River. Iveri's stories of his childhood sounded very similar except that this was in Fiji. He comes from an Island where the teachers, doctors and lawyers came from and then worked across the 326 small islands of Fiji. Naturally, he has a very deep speaker's voice and a calm personality. Before he joined the British Army, Iveri was a well-respected primary teacher in Fiji. His students really liked him, he was an authority in his field, and he was an amateur rugby player. If you have not met a Fijian before, these guys are naturally fit in build and size with strong bones and large shoulders.

In 1961, a pivotal moment in history unfolded as the British Army opened its doors to a new wave of recruits from the distant shores of Fiji. This was a time when the island nation was still a Crown Colony, and the call to serve resonated deeply within its people. Among the first to answer this call was Maikeli Vuli, a young Fijian man whose journey would take him far from the sun-drenched beaches of his homeland. After completing his service, Maikeli made the city of Doncaster his new home, a testament to the enduring bonds forged between the Fijian people and the British military. Maikeli was not alone in this endeavour. He was part of a pioneering group of 212 Fijian men and women, hailing from diverse ethnic backgrounds, who were recruited into the British Army in that fateful year of 1961. Their bravery and dedication would soon be put to the test, as one of their own, Sergeant Talaiasi Labalaba, found himself in the thick of the Battle of Mirbat just over a decade later. This historic recruitment drive, orchestrated by the British Armed Forces, was a critical juncture that forever intertwined the fates of Fiji and the United Kingdom. It marked the beginning of a long tradition of Fijian participation in the British military, a tradition that continues to this day. As the years passed, many of these Pacific Islanders, affectionately known as the "212," chose to make the United Kingdom their permanent home, weaving their rich cultural tapestry into the fabric of British society. Their stories, like that of Maikeli Vuli, serve as a testament to the resilience, courage, and unwavering spirit that defined this pioneering generation of Fijian soldiers. In the annals of history, the year 1961 will forever be etched as the moment when the bonds between Fiji and the British Army were forged, a bond that has withstood the test of time and continues to strengthen with each passing generation.

Iveri politely introduced himself and his first-born son who was twice the height of him. Iveri, like most Fijians I had the pleasure to meet and speak with, told me a different story. This was his second attempt to join the British Army, having failed in 2003 due to lack of a sponsor. Now, in 2006, he clutched a letter inviting him to the selection process, his dream of becoming an army medic within reach. The journey from his home on Kadavu Island to Suva had been arduous. It began with a long walk, followed by a boat ride to the mainland, and finally a bus trip to the capital. The entire trek took five hours, reminiscent of a complex journey from the Isle of Wight to London, but at a much slower pace typical of remote Fiji. Fortunately, Iveri wasn't alone; his nephew and brother-in-law who were also invited to the selection process, accompanied him on his quest. The next day dawned with English and Maths exams administered by the British Army recruitment team who had travelled for 24 hours to conduct this exercise in Fiji. This wasn't the first time such recruitment had been carried out to bolster UK Forces from the Colonies and wider Commonwealth. In the afternoon, the infamous fitness test loomed. The mile-and-a-half run had to be completed in under 9 minutes, but expectations were higher for those under 21 – under 8 minutes was the unofficial benchmark for peak fitness. Iveri, with his teaching background, had his heart set on the Medical Corps. However, his recruiter steered him towards the Rifles instead, assuring him he could transfer after basic training. This scenario was all too common for thousands of Fijians and Commonwealth recruits joining the British Army – the trap of being unable to change trade or regiment once enlisted. Iveri, like many others, found himself at the mercy of recruiters who were incentivised to fill specific regiments, regardless of the recruit's preferences. As Iveri contemplated his future in the Rifles, he couldn't help but wonder about the path ahead. Would he be able to pursue his dream of becoming a medic? Or would he, like so many before him, find himself locked into a role he hadn't initially chosen? Despite these uncertainties, the promise of a new life and opportunities in the British Army propelled him forward, ready to face whatever challenges lay ahead.

Iveri stood at the edge of his farm, the sun setting over the lush Fijian landscape. This was the second time he was applying to join the British Army and, without a sponsor, the path ahead required him to be entirely self-sufficient. In the UK, a sponsor is someone who takes full responsibility for you, proving they can accommodate, feed, and support you during the recruitment process. But Iveri had no such sponsor. Fiji is about 9,750 miles from the UK, and the journey is not just physically demanding but financially draining. Flights are costly and the living expenses in the UK add up quickly. For Iveri, this was a monumental sacrifice. He was married and a father, and for a Fijian to join the British Army was a significant investment. It wasn't about severing ties with his homeland but rather about building a bridge for others to follow or at least being able to send something back home. When a Fijian family sends a son or daughter to join the British Army, it's akin to putting money away for a pension. If you don't have the savings, those who invest in you expect a return. For Iveri, this meant sacrificing some of his land and farm business. In Fiji, most families have farms to grow fruits, vegetables, and cattle for their own sustenance, with any excess sold at the marketplace. Iveri needed $15,000 (roughly £5,000), to be self-sufficient. Many of his British colleagues had no idea of the sacrifices Fijians made to join the British Armed Forces. They often assumed Fijians were homeless, shirtless, and without prospects back home. But those who took the time to listen, perhaps during long night watches at the gates or during operations like Op Telic and Op Herrick, became lifelong supporters. Life on the frontline in the heat of battle forged incredible bonds. The biggest challenge for most Fijian soldiers was staying in contact with loved ones back home. Before the days of WhatsApp and Messenger, they relied on Calling Cards, which cost £5 each and provided 60 minutes of talk time. Some resorted to writing letters due to the lack of communication options. When Iveri finally arrived in the UK, he was fortunate to stay with friends and joined The Rifles. Though he was never allowed to change regiments, he had no regrets. "I had a great time with The Rifles," he often said, reflecting on the camaraderie and experiences that shaped his journey.

Chapter Twenty-Four

Africa Day

One might easily confuse Africa Day with Commonwealth Day. What is Africa Day and how did this come about?

Africa has always been close to my heart. When you are born on an island 30 x 60 km and raised among many Afro-Mauritians (also known as Creole Mauritians), you are bound to feel part of the big continent or at least wonder what life is like in Africa. By the time I was 19, I had left Mauritius to visit Africa. For Mauritians when we lift or heads to the sky, we don't see Europe but we see Africa.

From a European standpoint, the era of colonialism left an indelible mark on the African continent, as European powers sought to tighten their grip and assert control over vast swathes of land and people. While the specific number of colonies is difficult to quantify, the impact was far-reaching and profound. For Britain, Kenya has always been a solid part of the colonial history. During the latter half of the 19th century, a wave of colonial expansion swept across Africa. This period, known as the "Scramble for Africa," saw European nations rush to claim territories, often with little regard for the wishes or wellbeing of the indigenous populations. The arbitrary drawing of borders by colonial powers sliced through ethnic, linguistic, and cultural lines, sowing the seeds of future conflict. As the 20th century dawned, the majority of the African continent found itself under the yoke of colonial rule. From the shores of West Africa to the vastness of the Great Lakes region, the resounding cries of subjugated peoples echoed across the land. The British Empire, with its sprawling network of colonies and protectorates, held sway over much of this narrative. In the decades that followed, a groundswell of resistance and liberation movements arose, fuelled by a yearning for self-determination and freedom from colonial oppression. The very idea of independence, once a mere whisper, grew into a deafening roar that could no longer be ignored. It was in this crucible of struggle that new nations were forged, their identities shaped by the resilience and perseverance of their people. From the ashes of colonialism, a renaissance of African pride and cultural renaissance took root, celebrating the rich tapestry of diversity that had been suppressed for too long. As we reflect on this chapter of history, we must remember the resilience of those who fought for their freedom and honour the sacrifices made in pursuit of a better future. For it was through their unwavering spirit that the chains of colonialism were broken, paving the way for the vibrant, independent nations that now grace the African continent.

Every year on 25 May, Africa and the global African diaspora come together to celebrate Africa Day – a commemoration that holds deep historical and cultural significance. Originally known as African Freedom Day and African Liberation Day, this occasion marks the founding of the Organisation of African Unity (OAU) in 1963, a pivotal moment in the continent's journey towards unity and self-determination. The formation of the OAU was a culmination of the Pan-African movement, a powerful intellectual, cultural, and political force that dates back to the 19th century. Pan-Africanism, at its core, is a worldview that emphasises the unity of the African continent and its peoples, advocating for their collective advancement in political, cultural, and economic spheres. As we celebrate the 54th anniversary of the OAU's transformation into the present-day African Union (AU), Africa Day provides an opportunity to reflect on the achievements of the Pan-African movement at national, regional, and continental levels. It is a time to pay tribute to the legacy and values of the founding fathers who laid the foundation for a united Africa, free from the shackles of colonial rule. Moreover, this celebration serves as a reminder to look ahead and accelerate socio-economic integration across the continent, asserting Africa's rightful place on the global stage. Fittingly, the theme for this year's Africa Day pays homage to African youth, recognising them as "the driving force behind the economic prosperity of the coming decades." The roots of this momentous occasion can be traced back to the aftermath of World War 2, when the process of decolonization gained momentum across the African continent. In 1945, the historic Fifth Pan-African Congress was held in Manchester, England, bringing together influential intellectuals and activists who would later become leaders in various African independence movements, including Kwame Nkrumah of Ghana and Jomo Kenyatta of Kenya. This pivotal congress marked a turning point in the Pan-African movement, demanding an end to decades of colonial rule and racial discrimination. The manifesto issued by the congress called for human rights, economic equality, and a new era of international cooperation, laying the foundation for the eventual liberation of African nations. As we celebrate Africa Day, we honour the sacrifices and struggles of those who came before us, while also looking towards a future where the African continent and its people can thrive and prosper, united in their diversity and rich cultural heritage.

Africa Day in the UK is likely celebrated through community cultural events, music and dance performances, academic programmes, and gatherings organised by diaspora groups to honour African unity, identity and liberation from colonial rule. However, the exact scale and nature of these celebrations across the UK is unclear.

The bond between the United Kingdom and the African continent is a tapestry woven with threads of history, colonialism, and evolving dynamics. This relationship, which spans centuries, has been shaped by both triumphs and challenges, leaving an indelible mark on the lives of countless individuals and nations. In the past, the UK's presence in Africa was marked by a colonial legacy that cast a long shadow. As the winds of change swept across the continent in the 1960s, African nations began to assert their independence, straining relations with their former colonial rulers. Prime Minister Harold Macmillan's famous "Winds of Change" speech in 1960 acknowledged this shifting reality, signalling the need for a new approach to the UK's engagement with Africa. In the years following decolonisation, the relationship between the UK and African nations ebbed and flowed, with periods of close engagement punctuated by times of relative neglect. However, under the leadership of Tony Blair and Gordon Brown from 1997 to 2010, a renewed focus on Africa emerged. This period saw an increase in aid, support for initiatives like NEPAD, and a heightened attention to African issues at G8 summits. Yet, as the tides of political priorities shifted once again after 2010, the relationship faded somewhat, with the UK Government turning its attention to other pressing matters such as the complexities of Brexit. Despite these fluctuations, the economic ties between the UK and Africa have remained a constant thread. The UK stands as one of the top investors in the South African economy and a major trade partner with many African nations. However, there is a recognition that these economic ties could be further strengthened and diversified, unlocking new opportunities for growth and prosperity on both sides. Moreover, the flow of remittances from the UK to African countries, particularly to nations like Nigeria, has become a lifeline, exceeding official development assistance flows and underscoring the deep connections between diaspora communities and their homelands. As the world evolves, so too must the relationship between the UK and Africa. Recent reports and initiatives, such as the 2020 House of Lords report and the UK-Africa Investment Summit, have underscored the need for a more strategic and balanced partnership – a call to action that emphasises clear priorities, improved visa processes, engagement with diaspora communities, and collaboration on pressing issues like debt, climate change, and trade relation. Yet, there is a growing recognition that this bond must be nurtured and strengthened, rooted in mutual respect, sustainable development, and a shared commitment to a brighter future for all.

In April 2022, the UK and Rwanda signed an agreement known as the 'Migration and Economic Partnership', or 'Rwanda Plan', for the UK to deport people seeking asylum to Rwanda. In November 2023, the UK Supreme Court ruled the plan to be unlawful as deporting migrants to Rwanda would breach British and international human rights laws and agreements. In response, the Prime Minister agreed a new treaty with Rwanda and brought forward new legislation – The Safety of Rwanda (Asylum and Immigration) Act – designed to override any legal obstacles and declared the country to be safe.

As social arms for Commonwealth soldiers and veterans in Aldershot Garrison, however, I see international events like Africa Day, as an opportunity to belong. So, in collaboration with the Rushmoor Cultural Event, I organised our third main event after Commonwealth Day with the sponsorship of Farnborough Football Club who kindly gave us its venue for the whole afternoon of 25 May. This event also coincided with Councillor Mara Makunura being elected as the first ever female Black Mayor with an African background. This was a huge event for Rushmoor County Council which is also the home of the British Army. This was the first time Rushmoor had such a well-attended event: we had people join us from Africa, the Caribbean, India and the Fiji Islands. In contrast with other Colonies like the French or the Spanish, Britain has the strongest pool of African countries through its Empire history and should leverage this in a positive way to help the African diaspora in the UK to belong.

Epilogue

The Danger in the Movement of People

In 1833, a time when Britain was in full control of India, they invented a new movement of people called Indentured Labourers. It was during this time also that slavery was abolished where the British Navy played a big part in stopping it, as I have evidenced earlier on in this book. It was then that the indentured labourers started. Between 1834 and 1920, over 2 million Indian indentured labourers were transported to various British, French, Dutch, and Danish colonies, including the Caribbean, Mauritius, Fiji, and South Africa. This was the first time in history that around two million South Asians were uprooted from their homeland in India with a promise of a better life. This episode in history is why we have South Asians across the Commonwealth today. It crept up on me – this feeling that we have a symptom and at the same time a cause across Britain. The symptom is the way that some people were treated which is deeply rooted in the past and the cause is based on a perception. Someone once said, 'a people without the knowledge of their past history, origin and culture is like a tree without roots.' Having now lived most of my adult life in Britain, I have come to realise that to be British is to always carry a sense of the past. Go anywhere in Britain and you can almost live in the shoe of someone who has lived here before you. I find this amazing.

I was once told by a lovely old English lady who happened to have been an earlier mayor, 'I always thought Commonwealth soldiers only served in WW2.' This made me realise that very few people outside the wire know of our existence – very few. However, inside the wire, Mike who is a professional CV writer, says: 'I heard a lot of prejudices against the Commonwealth soldiers. Some would say, "they can't even speak

English properly" while others would say, "they are only here for the passport".'

This book is not about citizenship. Everyone who has worn a British uniform feels British, although the reality can be deceiving for many after giving their service. This is not about allegiance. Most Commonwealth individuals I know are loyal to King and Country. This is not about where we call home - why would someone join the British military and be ready to die for a country if they have no interest in belonging to British society and integrating in the community? It is easy to write about racism or prejudices – although according to Robert Ford, more and more people are now in contact with a Black and Brown person.

I chuckled to myself, thinking of the unspoken message I had learned to convey over the years:

"Don't worry about my brown skin colour. I'm here to help, not to threaten." It was a delicate balance, being both visibly different and reassuringly familiar. I think I have been conditioned by the art of British manners – politeness, harmless banter in the military, at universities where I lecture, in the pub for a meal, in the public space where you make small talk, and countless other social settings – where you learn to send the subliminal message: 'Don't worry about the fact that I am brown, I won't make you feel uncomfortable. I may be brown, bald headed and have a somehow difficult name to pronounce, but it's OK – I am on your side, I will do anything to respect you rather than threatening you. I am brown, and speak with an accent, but safe'. I believe this is the message that most Commonwealth and Gurkhas walking in our street today would like to say to Britain.

As I reflect on the journey through this book, I realise that it's been shaped not just by historical events but by the lived experiences of hundreds of Commonwealth veterans in the UK. Their stories have been the heart of this narrative. While it may be tempting to end with a forward-looking perspective, the real power lies in understanding where we've been. By examining these personal accounts and the policies that have affected them, we can gain valuable insights into our current situation and potential future directions. It's crucial to recognise that healing can only begin once wrongs have been openly acknowledged and owned. Change requires a clear articulation of what needs to be transformed. In today's political climate, with the rising influence of anti-immigrant parties across Europe, Commonwealth veterans often find themselves unfairly categorised and discriminated against simply because they may look or sound like immigrants. Another challenge we face is the tendency for groups to focus solely on their issues rather than addressing broader, systemic problems. Finding meaningful dialogue between different Commonwealth groups about shared challenges is rare. Paradoxically, our progress in some areas has become part of the problem. The systemic racism towards Commonwealth people in Britain will only indeed fade when we confront the profoundly ingrained 'Windrushian mentality' that has conditioned people within these systems for generations. This is why we need to re-examine the Commonwealth experience in Britain, the process that has underpinned life of Commonwealth veterans after giving their service in Britain for the best part of 80 years. We need to accept that a part of the way in which it has been implanted, may have delivered something we never envisaged or intended. To ignore the lessons detailed in this book risks creating a backlash that might unhinge everything that has been achieved from 1944 to 2024, quickly cascading into yet another Windrushian scandal across Britain.

To move forward, Britain must continue to share these stories, challenge discriminatory policies, and work towards processes with principles that recognise the valuable contributions of all its members, regardless of their origins.

As for the Commonwealth people in Britain, we come from many different races and origins, encompass every state of economic development, and comprise a rich variety of cultures, traditions and institutions. This is very distinct from other international organisations like the World Trade Organisation and the United Nations. This lacks written rules and a constitution. Our group's members are bound together by common customs, institutions and experiences, as well as economic self-interest; we do not have a formal or legal commitment to one another but we do have our common experience. Whilst Commonwealth citizens were heavily recruited in Fiji, Africa and the Caribbeans by the British Army after 2000, surprisingly there is very little mentioned of this in Britain – not in the papers or in any online media – which is very strange because how can you have thousands of Commonwealth soldiers with their families living in Britain and in overseas British camps with so very little knowledge about us by the British population we are serving?

As I finish this book, I am putting teams, ambassadors and partners across Britain to support Op Belonging works to ensure that those who have risked their lives for this country feel valued and supported, both during their service and after transition to civilian life. Only by fostering meaningful connections and providing access to various support services can we together reinvent the Commonwealth experience in Britain and I invite you to join me and the thousands before me on this journey.

You can download the Op Belonging App on your phone by visiting www.OpBelonging.com to talk to my team directly, and I look forward meeting you at one of my events on 'Building Bridges, Fostering Belonging' which are being held across the UK.

Yours,
SamuelTReddy.com

About the Authors

Born in Mauritius, made in Britain, Samuel T. Reddy is an authority in career transition and bestselling author of the book 'Leavers to Leaders'. He has a track record of solving complex organisational problems through human capital solutions. Through his career and leadership accredited transition programme, he helps people and organisations make sure that their next move is the best move.

Professor Martin Levermore MBE, a child of the Windrush generation, is the Chief Executive of Medical Devices Technology International, a member of the pioneer team (the Health Data hub for acute care), a serial entrepreneur and Deputy Lieutenant of the West Midlands.

Also by Samuel T. Reddy:

Leavers to Leaders
Reinvented
7 Career Transition Mistakes To Avoid

Connect with Samuel

 www.linkedin.com/in/samueltreddy
 SamuelTReddy
samueltreddy
 www.OpBelonging.com
www.SamuelTReddy.com

Printed in Great Britain
by Amazon